What makes this book uniqu̲ estate agents. However, we h̲ the lives of the real estate agent because of our education, background and extensive experience working with some of the most successful agents in the business. Where somebody in the real estate business might interact with a handful of real estate professionals over the course of the year, we're interacting with hundreds or thousands of them over hundreds of thousands of transactions over a long period of time. This unique perspective provides insight and information that's valuable to both real estate professionals that are struggling and the agents who are successful and want to take their business to the next level.
- Chad Hett

SECRETS OF TOP PRODUCING REAL ESTATE AGENTS

And How To Duplicate Their Success

Over 50 years' experience in real estate and 400,000 agents have gone into making this book!

Chad Hett
Jase Souder
Ken Sherman

Dedication

This book is dedicated to all of the hard-working
and dedicated entrepreneurs,
real estate professionals and self-made business owners.

You *can* become your best - who you know you've always been
meant to be - your best and the best in your field!

Contents

Acknowledgments

We would like to thank our family and friends for their love and support, without you none of this would be possible

Introduction

**A CEO, a Sales Coach, and an Authority Marketing
Consultant pull back the curtain on over 400,000
transactions and share what it takes to be a successful real
estate agent.**

Inside this book, you'll get their secret view of what makes
most agents fail, and how to avoid it. You'll also learn what it
takes to achieve and excel as a real estate professional from
two people who have a unique view of the
real estate world: the CEO of the largest privately held home
inspection company in North America, a company which has
seen over 350,000 transactions and a top sales trainer who has
over a decade of coaching and speaking for agents and
entrepreneurs. You'll also gain powerful insights from an
authority marketing and positioning expert on how to build
instant credibility for clients using many of the same
techniques used by celebrity entrepreneurs.

About The Authors

Meet Chad Hett

I'm co-owner of The Elite Group Property Inspections based in California. I'm also a family man with a passion for business; a guy who has proven that I understand the nuts and bolts of how to drive business. My thirst for success and the knowledge of what makes people successful keeps me busy studying, learning and attending seminar after seminar to continually improve myself and my business.

Over 20 years ago, after graduating from San Diego State University, I began my career in the real estate/property inspection business. While many businesses were struggling through the recent economic downturn, my business grew by leaps and bounds. By applying simple principles of doing business the right way, I was able to grow several companies many times over.

As a business owner, I've learned how critical it is to not become complacent and expect business just to come in. The successful business professional goes after business with a hunger and keeps the competition from chipping away at their success. Success takes a continued commitment to always be improving, to providing superior customer services, and to being the best you can be; dotting every 'I,' crossing every 'T'. This mindset of entrepreneurship brings the confidence and security that completely separates you from any competition whatsoever.

What makes this book unique is that none of the authors are real estate agents. However, we have a unique perspective into the lives of the real estate agent because of our education, background and extensive experience working with some of the most successful agents in the business. Where somebody in the real estate business might interact with a handful of real estate professionals over the course of the year, we're interacting with hundreds or thousands of them over hundreds of thousands of transactions over a long period of time. This unique perspective provides insight and information that's valuable to both real estate professionals that are struggling and the agents who are successful and want to take their business to the next level.

As co-owner at The Elite Group Property Inspections, where we do 15,000 + inspections a year I have spent years working with agents. My home inspection company has done over 350,000 inspections. That means 350,000 times my company has met with buyer's agents or listing agents to go do an inspection. We regularly meet with buyers and sellers and are involved in sales transactions every day. In fact, we've been in contact with over 500,000 agents over time.

This unique perspective gives us insight into how the most successful real estate professionals create success; what they do daily and how they conduct their business, what their mindset is, how they think about their business, etc. We see what sets the top 20% of agents apart from the bottom 80%.

We also see many agents that are just stumbling through their real estate career. We see them once every 3 months or so. They're always down...their head is not completely in the business.

Over time, we've also worked closely and have established relationships with many of the top selling real estate professionals...the top 10%. We've learned from both types of agent about what it takes to be successful in the real estate business, not just in real estate, but in business in general. I've successfully implemented many of the powerful strategies outlined in this book into my own businesses throughout the years. My business continues to grow as a direct result of my own personal development, coaching, sales training and improved communication skills.

I wanted to be involved in writing this book because what I know about how the best of the best agents operate will help other real estate agents, the bottom 80%, to achieve more.

About The Elite Group Property Inspections

As the largest independently owned home inspection agency in North America, The Elite Group is dedicated to providing quality services in line with our motto, "Inspecting to a higher standard since 1984." A passion for excellence has made The Elite Group Property Inspections the inspection agency of choice for many of the top brokers and real estate agents in Los Angeles, Orange County, Riverside County, San Bernardino County, San Diego, Sacramento, and surrounding areas. Our seasoned agents have inspected more than 350,000 homes. In fact, we've completed more home inspections than any other inspection company in California. For more information about The Elite Group Property Inspections please visit their website online at: http://www.eliteinspections.com/.

Meet Jase Souder

The reason I do all of it...my 'Why' is that I believe our businesses aren't just where we make money; they're where we make a difference.

I believe we all have a God-given mission, that only we can do, and it can be fulfilled and funded through our businesses.

My personal mission in life is to help you fulfill your mission. I believe that the more good people who have money, the more good things will happen in our world. Today, success and money buy influence, and in America we especially need more good people to have more influence. I really believe through the individual entrepreneur, we can make the world a better place, and if America has any hopes of a middle class, it's through small-business.

As a trainer, I've seen the difference in the people that succeed and the people that don't and what skills they're missing. I travel the country learning what makes entrepreneurs successful and then bring it to my presentations to help agents achieve more. For well over a decade, I've been training real estate agents, real estate investors, entrepreneurs and small to large size businesses. A couple of years ago, I did an 11,000-mile, 18-city speaking tour that was predominantly for real estate professionals. Facilitating sales training presentations with nothing but real estate agents in the room, I got to know about agents and their business at a deep level.

I'm passionate about this book because I've lived the journey from barely making it as an agent to having great success in business. My perspective comes from a guy who has lived it and from that of a coach and speaker who does in-field training to give agents the no-holds-barred, real true story of what they need, and a business owner that interacts with thousands of small business owners every year as an educator an advocate for their success.

I was a struggling agent - I knew I could do better, much better, and it wasn't until a Sales Trainer stepped into my life and made a difference, by showing me that I could do it, and how to do it, that my life took off. I remember what it was like to feel like I was made for more and just get down and depressed by just not achieving what I knew I could. It wasn't until I learned how to change the way I think, how I thought of myself, and more importantly, learned how to sell, that I began to see the results I wanted to produce. I learned to not only sell others on my services and products; I learned to sell myself on myself.

What caused me to change? I was desperate.

I was just *done* with who I'd been and how my life was, and I made the commitment to change no matter what. In 2001, I was a real estate professional and an investor when 9/11 hit and I used it as an excuse to tank my life. Between 9/11 and the next 6 months I made a total of $2,000 in commission. $2000 in 6 months...my life just wasn't working. It just wasn't the way I wanted it to be, I knew I was made to do more in life.

I'd see these other people who were just making tons of money and I wasn't, and it was really frustrating; some of my fellow agents made more between 9/11 and the end of the year than they'd made the previous 9 months.

I asked myself, "How did they do it," and "What do they know that I don't, or what's different about them, what qualities do they have that I don't?"

I was attending seminars on improving my business, but something was missing. One day I saw a speaker and he talked about making more money, but none of what he said was about how to be a better agent. He said that for me to make more money I needed to change my thinking and I needed to learn to sell.

I went to his seminar and it changed my life: I got my dreams back, I began to believe I was worthy of success, and I learned to sell. When I purchased his program it came with a home study course on sales and I devoured it. I listened to it multiple times!

The more I learned about improving myself and how to sell, the happier I was and the more money I made. I had found what I needed to change my life for the better, and I started going to personal development seminars and learning sales. The personal development seminars changed my life, got me motivated, and the sales training helped me get more clients and change their lives, too.

I started attending every sales training and personal development event that I could find - I was determined to change myself for the better - I even went to training on how to eat properly at a business meeting! I started investing more and more money in personal development, and sales training, I hired a coach and I got even more motivated.

At one of the personal development seminars I found my passion for speaking, educating and entertaining. I had changed my life and I wanted to help others do the same.

The reason I wanted to be involved in this book is that I know what it's like to be that agent who's struggling. I know what it's like to be that business owner who has talent, has a mission in life and who just isn't achieving it.

I believe anybody can be a success; and that it's a matter of training and development. It's a matter of changing your subconscious programming and learning to sell more by using some of the tools and keys we'll talk about in this book. I believe across any industry, these techniques and practices will work for any business owner, and they were originally created to help the real estate professionals.

I've lived the story of putting into place what we're teaching. When I was a struggling agent, I used to hear people say, "You should go visit 'For Sale By Owners' and call them up and see if they will list."

I didn't know how to sell and I was so afraid of rejection. Fearfully, I might call them once and if they said no, I'd tell myself, "Every 'no' you get leads you closer to a 'yes.' I got that 'no' out of the way."

They say that you can typically close 10% of the people out there if you're decent at selling. The truth is if you stink you'll get 10% of the people. If you're absolutely horrible, but you call enough people, you'll close one out of 10.

If you're good at sales though, and if you're persistent and effective, and you apply the principles outlined in this book, you could close 4, 5, 6, 7 or even 8 out of 10 (if you're closing 9 out of 10, call me, I want to interview you for my next book). You'll never get 10 out of 10, but you can close a lot more.

Knowing I needed to be better at selling, I started going to training seminars and workshops. I was investing a significant amount of money and my time was stretched thin because a lot of the events were out of town.

Where I used to call a 'for sale by owner' once, I now needed to make more money because I was spending all my money on these workshops. Now instead of just calling them just once, I actually called them back. If they said 'no' or 'not right now,' I'd say, 'Awesome, I'll follow up again soon' and I call them back again.

What I discovered was when I kept in touch, was persistent in a nice way and I kept calling back, I got more people to list with me. I actually had less time, I was busier, and I made way more money because I didn't have time to waste.

I wouldn't just be sitting around the office and messing around on the computer. I'd actually be calling the people I needed to call and I'd say, "Hey, do you want to work together? Not yet? Great, I'll call you later." I'd keep calling or visiting them and I'd pick up way more listings and way more buyers.

I think the prospects could feel my energy. They could feel I was more positive. They could feel I wanted to get it done. People can sense those subconscious emotions, the unspoken things, so they'd work with me.

Science is proving this true today - organizations such as the Heart Math Institute are discovering that the heart gives off an electromagnetic field 5,000 times more powerful than the brain. I was motivated, you might say, "On fire," and people could feel it, so I attracted motivated people.

I didn't have time in my life anymore for the tire-kickers and buyers and the prospects who were just thinking about it, because those weren't going to close. They could feel it too, and either got motivated or got gone.

I needed to get people who were ready to buy now. The people who wanted to buy now, and who wanted to work with an agent who wanted to help them now. Listings who were motivated wanted to work with me because I was an agent who would do what it took to get the listing sold.

By me shifting how I showed up in the game, the game got a lot better for me.

You can do this. You are good enough, you were born by God to be something special, and there's a mission only you can fulfill. If you're willing to trust, keep going and move beyond what you've known of yourself, others and business, you too can become who you've always wanted to be.

I'll close this introduction and open the door to this book and your new life with this: you're going to face fear and resistance. To help you beat them I want to share a saying that works for me when I'm facing growth, and the accompanying fear and resistance,

"Say 'Yes' and take a step!"

When you don't think you can: say "Yes" and take a step, any step you can toward your destination.
When you don't know how it will turn out you're gripped by fear, say "Yes" and take a step.

When you don't know if they'll say, "Yes" or if you're good enough, just say "Yes" and take a step. Do the next thing you can.

Say "Yes" and take a step enough times and you'll be exactly where you want to be.

Your next yes is to this book, and your next step is to turn the page.

- Jase Souder

About Jase Souder

Jase Souder is a nationally recognized public speaker and trainer, specializing in sales, marketing, mindset and public speaking, which helps entrepreneurs find success, influence and productivity.

Jase has appeared on national and local TV and radio and he's in the inspirational movies *Pass It On* and *The Power of Coaching* where he's featured along with Brian Tracy, John Assaraf, Rev. Michael Beckwith, Boxing Champion Evander Holyfield, Rudy Ruettiger, Les Brown and many of today's thought leaders.

Jase is the creator of the Persuasion Paradigm, an effective step-by-step influence system, the DYSALA Healing Method and is the founder of Life Tigers LLC, a leading personal development seminar company.   A bestselling author, Jase is in four bestselling books.

Jase is an in demand Keynote Speaker, Trainer and Entertainer, appearing at venues from the small business owner to Fortune 50 companies.

For more information about Jase Souder, please visit his website at: http://www.jasesouder.com/.

Meet Ken Sherman

I am the owner of an authority internet marketing agency, GoProLocal. I help entrepreneurs and business professionals to differentiate themselves in their market from their competition-to become the obvious choice among their prospects and customers.

My background as an entrepreneur and multi-business owner allow me to serve my clients from a unique perspective of marketing consultant and fellow business owner.

I went to college at Arizona State University and graduated with an Aeronautic Engineering degree in 1993, just in time for the whole airline industry to collapse and the job market to dry up in my field of study.

Instead of Aeronautic Engineering, I started a specialized cleaning company in Arizona. I worked with home owners and real estate agents and investors doing fix/flips directly as a trusted contractor resource. Very quickly I realized that the opportunity to be a leader in the home service industry was in my future.

I put up a website for my service business early on and very quickly I got a phone call from a man in Chicago named Mike. He said, *'I'm on your website and I'd like to come to Phoenix to learn how to do what you do. I have a handyman business. I want to add what you do to my list of services; how much to teach me?'*

We negotiated a price that I never imagined he'd pay and he asked me if I preferred a cashier's check on arrival or if he should mail me the funds in advance. I was blown away.

My website, on this new thing called the internet, just made me a ridiculously large sum of money. Mike flew out the next week, helped me on my jobs for four days while I coached him on selling my services and how to position himself in his market. He went back to Chicago to be hugely successful, even spinning off a whole new standalone specialty company.

I talked to Mike a few years later and learned that what I had taught him to do had completely changed his life. What he told me that day changed mine.

He explained that what I showed him brought the financial independence that allowed him to provide for his family in a way he never imagined possible. He told me about several family vacations that he'd taken that he'd never forget, and that he was able to pay his son's college tuition in full. Then he thanked me for sharing my expertise those years ago and that it meant a lot to him.... I nearly teared up on the phone.

When I asked Mike why he chose me to come to for training, he said, "Because you're an expert, and I wanted to learn from the best."

The Authority Positioning seeds were firmly planted in my brain at that point. To think that I could make a difference like that in someone's life inspired me at a very deep level. I found that I enjoy the role of educator and advocate and embraced a philosophy of helping people and solving problems. And to know his decision was influenced by how I had positioned myself online was a turning point.

In the years since I've spoken with Mike, my company has trained hundreds of contractors from around the world offering innovative and industry leading training opportunities. My training course even became certified for continuing education credit by the Institute of Inspection,

Cleaning and Restoration (IICRC). Once again, my team and I were positioned as industry leaders. And that just led to more success.

All these years later, we're now a leading manufacturer of innovative cleaning products, training programs and business building resources used by contractors worldwide in the flooring restoration industry.

Once I realized how powerful position is I began studying how celebrity entrepreneurs were positioning themselves in the media. I learned everything I could about internet marketing; an educational journey that I continue to enjoy some 20+ years later.

With today's technology, many of the techniques used by the entertainment industry to build celebrity are readily available to the public. These days, I use technology to help businesses of all types open up new channels of revenue by using authority marketing and expert online positioning to become the leader that their prospects want to work with.

 Most of the business professionals I work with are already successful...and being successful, they want more success. I'm able to come in and say, 'Look, here's what we can do to showcase you and your business as the obvious choice among your prospects and customers and help you close more business. The outside perspective and expertise I bring to business professionals and entrepreneurs is valuable and effective.

Internet Marketing Educator, Jack Mize, always says, "Make more doing less." That hits home for me. I tell my clients, "Focus in on something that you're good at and stick with that. Work in your talent area and you will see amazing success in your business."

I help business professionals and entrepreneurs to expand their reach, open new doors of opportunity, charge more for their services and be sought after by prospects.

 I wanted to be a part of this book because I know how important establishing yourself as "the authority" in your field is to achieving success in business. Too many real estate professionals are stuck in the day to day of running their business and they are missing out on a lot of opportunity because they don't understand how to position themselves as an expert and an authority at what they do.

Being seen as the go to person in your local area or industry leads to a much easier sales process no matter what business you're in; especially in real estate.

About Ken Sherman and GoProLocal

GoProLocal specializes in authority marketing and authority positioning. Their services include personal branding, online search engine optimization and Internet marketing strategies. Ken explains, "Our specialty is helping business owners and professionals increase their bottom line by positioning them and their business as an industry leader—an authority in their market."

Managing Director, Ken Sherman is an Amazon multiple best-selling author and an entrepreneur with a passion for taking action and overcoming obstacles. He's an effective team builder and excellent communicator with a strong ability to take ideas from concept to completion. Ken has been quoted in the national media as an expert in authority marketing and online authority positioning and serves as a passionate educator and advocate for his prospects and clients.

For more information about Ken Sherman and GoProLocal visit: http://www.AuthorityPosition.com.

SECTION 1: PREPARATION

We're going to start this book by preparing the most important part of your business for success: you.

If an agent is not prepared to succeed, they can be given the best sales and marketing tools in the world and they will still fail. Think about it, if you give someone the key to the door of riches, and all they have to do to get what they want in business is to go to the door, put the key in, unlock and open the door - yet they have no intention to open the door, they don't make the time, they lack the desire or think they're unable to do it, they'll never open the door. Your time and effort will be wasted.

If you give a prepared person the same key, the door will be opened and they'll have a new life.

The first section of this book is to assist you in being the person who will take the keys we're going to give you and unlock the doors to success.

This book has been written in 3 sections:
Preparation
Positioning
Profit

Preparation is about preparing you for success.

Positioning is about how to position yourself in the market, so you're chosen by your prospects to be their agent.

Profit is putting it all together, and learning the one skill that will determine the failure, or success, of your company.

Chapter 1:
The Ineffective Agent

The Ineffective Agent
In real estate, you've got so many hardworking people making a mediocre income. According to the Bureau of Labor Statistics, real estate agents earned a median salary of $40,990 in 2014. Only the top 10% earned more than $105,270 per year with only a very small percentage of agents making over $250,000 per year.
(http://www.bls.gov/oes/current/oes419022.htm)

What are the most successful agents doing?
What's the difference between an average agent and a super successful one?

As part of putting this book together, we talked with real estate office owners and brokers, and drew from our own experience to find the answer, and we discovered success in real estate is not about the tools and techniques of real estate.

What's the answer to the difference between the average agent and the super successful? Well, there's not just one, and there's a main one...

Ineffective Agents Carry a Negative Mindset

The biggest difference between the profitable agent and the unsuccessful is that the people who aren't successful don't believe "It" will work for them (whatever "It" it is), are naysayers, generally unpleasant and don't go for "it."

It's easy to identify the ineffective, negative mindset agent - they don't invest in themselves, and they're difficult to work with. The ones who don't succeed don't get coaching, they don't learn how to sell, they don't have a business plan and they don't have a consistent, empowering learning environment.

How to get over being an Ineffective Agent with a Negative Mindset: Get on fire or Get Desperate.

This is Jase, and in my opinion there are two types of people that are great with which to work: the on fire or the desperate.

The on fire are the ones who are doing great in business and they instantly and eagerly apply what they learn because they know training and development works, they know sales training works, they know the more tools and skills they get, the more success will follow. The on-fire people are involved, apply quickly and are happy and eager to pick up new tools, personal development and sales skills and use them fast. They're quick to buy personal development and sales training tools not because they have the extra money, they're quick because they know it works.

They don't invest in personal development and sales training because they have extra money. They have extra money *because* they invest in personal development and sales training.

The other agents I love to work with are the desperate; the ones who just can't seem to get it working, and know it. They're at the end of the rope and they know they've got to change something, "Or else." They know they have to change or die (well, at least their business will die).

The desperate have run out of options, and they know doing it their way doesn't work so they're willing to let go of what they've known and they're willing to try something new...and in doing something new, they'll find their success.

I love to work with the desperate because they're super motivated, willing to let go of the ways which don't work, don't argue, and apply the new ideas quickly. They'll invest because they have to, and they'll apply quickly because they must.

The soul crushing, dream killing, profit stealing agents: the "Comfortable" middle.
The agents who are difficult to work with are the ones in the middle: the ones in their, "Comfort zone." They're not hurting so bad they have to change, and they're definitely not doing great and applying fast. They're not really comfortable; their life is really like a low grade stink. Their life is called comfortable because they're not in so much pain they have to change.

I can't stand working, or I should say, attempting to work with these people. As a trainer I want to see people use my information and succeed, making their life and their family's life better. I do this work to make a difference. Working with the lukewarm middle is difficult because these people don't buy, don't apply and usually sit around and complain, and waste my time and efforts.

It turns out this philosophy is thousands of years old. There's a passage in a great book of wisdom that says, "So, because you are lukewarm--neither hot nor cold--I am about to spit you out of my mouth."

At speaking engagements, I can tell you who's who in the audience. It's the people who sit back with their arms closed— they're skeptical, closed off, have a bad look on their face, argue, resist and are difficult. I find they tend to make the least amount of money.

Where do you think the most successful people in the room sit? They sit right up front. In a learning environment they sit right in the front row, they're involved, they take notes, and they're open. The On Fire and Effective agents participate, smile, take notes, make encouraging comments and have compliments to give. I've seen this over and on my USA Victory Tour, where we trained agents all across the USA: the most successful agents, the brokers and owners who were succeeding sat right up front.

Ineffective Agents Don't Invest in Their Own Training and Coaching
Typically when I make an offer, most successful people in the room buy my trainings and products really fast. It's not that they buy because they're making money; they make money because they've learned to act fast. That type of quick decision making and action carries over to business: they see a for sale by owner (FSBO), and they call it quickly. They see an opportunity for improvement and they take it...and that kind of fast action leads to success.

Ineffective Agents Lack Self-Discipline and Emotional Management

Ineffective Agents let their personal life and challenges stop their business as they don't have the emotional self management to handle the setbacks, interruptions and resistance that is part of life, and especially part of growing a successful business. Because they don't know how to manage their emotions they bring a lot of drama to the office.

They don't have the self-discipline and the emotional management tools to get done what needs to get done regardless of circumstance. They have breakdowns in production and to cover up for their breakdowns they make excuses and blame others.

**SUCCESS TIP: If you see yourself as one of these, we recommend getting to a few good personal development seminars and read the book *Emotional Intelligence* by Daniel Goleman.

Ineffective Agents Don't Structure Their Day
Ineffective Agents don't have a schedule, so they either waste time (usually they waste not only their time, what's worse, they interrupt and lead astray other influence-able agents in the office - thereby pulling down the whole office) or they just run around putting out fires so that they feel like they accomplished something.

We understand that sometimes new agents just don't know what to do. They go in the office and they don't know where to start, and while they may be motivated, the lack of structure and guidance to make them effective. It's still no excuse.

If you're a new agent and you don't know what to do, and you're not getting guidance, you're at the wrong brokerage. At least you have this book. Let this book be your guide.

Ineffective Agents Quit Growing Because They Have a Sense of Entitlement and That They're Better Than Everyone Else

In life you're either growing or your dying. You're either learning, applying or putting energy into your life or your life is beginning to atrophy. This goes for your physical fitness, your income, relationships and your career.

If you own a plant, you understand this concept; you're either putting in what the plant needs for growth, like water, the right nutrients and energy or you leave it alone and it starts to wither.

Your business is the similar to a plant in that you either give it what it needs to grow or it's going to start dying. You can't just leave it alone without it starting to atrophy. Grow or die.

Our friend David Corbin said it best:
"You're either green and growing or ripe and rotten."

We've seen so many real estate professionals and brokers that feel entitled, like they are owed something by their office, other agents, and the rest of the world, or they feel like they're better than everyone else, at the top of their game and they know it all. When they are entitled or think they're better than anyone else, they're not open to training, they are a no to growth, they don't push to improve..and they get left behind.

They could have been great, instead they end up failing miserably because they lack the understanding of what it takes to maintain and advance themselves and their business in real and measurable ways.

Ineffective Agents can be Lazy

Another reason some agents are ineffective is just plain laziness; laziness in communication, in developing solid business systems, laziness in marketing themselves and positioning themselves as the #1 choice of their prospects, etc.

They lack the feeling of urgency that's required to really make it big in real estate. They fall behind further and further until they start looking for a new career.

Laziness can come in many forms including not getting it done, not growing, making excuses etc. These agents make excuses for why they can't learn new things, why they don't have the time for the important things that make average agents great, why they didn't get it done on time, and really, they make too many excuses for us to list here .

WARNING: If an agent is lazy, they shouldn't even be in real estate; it's just not going to work out for them.

Ineffective Agents Lack Sales Skills
Ineffective Agents don't know how to close, they don't know how to gain rapport, they don't know how to find motivation, they don't know how to talk on the phone, they don't know how to speak to personality types, they haven't learned scripts, and they don't know how to sell themselves on getting things done, so they get stuck by fear and often don't even ask for the deal.

Ineffective Agents Lack Good Communication
Good communication is a key skill that ineffective agents often lack. They either communicate in ways that kill deals, or they fail to follow through and communicate at crucial moments.

Ineffective Agents Are Derailed by Fear
Their fear manifests in making excuses. "Oh, I didn't have the time. I don't have the money. I don't want to call people. I don't have the (fill in the blank)."

Ineffective Agents Don't Consider the Human Aspects of Their Business
Ineffective Agents don't consider the human aspects of their business. They don't understand the huge responsibility, and rare opportunity to serve they have, when helping a client.

They don't see that being involved as a representative for a buyer or seller is a privilege.

To serve someone is not a right, it's a privilege and perhaps one of the best we can experience in life.

Ineffective Agents Lose Sight of the Owner's Investment of Time and Effort

Ineffective Agents discount their client's time end effort and only count their own.

For example: even if a seller owns a property outright, the ineffective agent doesn't consider that the owner very likely worked long and hard to be in that position.

Ineffective agents lose sight of the fact that the property owner sacrificed time with their family and friends by working late or on weekends, missing family trips and foregoing things they'd like to pursue all just to make that mortgage payment. Property owners put a lot of trust in an agent and rely on the agent they choose to respect the years they spent to get where they are.

Ineffective Agents Fail Because of:

* Wrong Mindset
* Lack of Training/Coaching
* Lack of Self-Discipline
* No Structure to the Day
* Feel Entitled/Better than Others
* Laziness
* Lack of Sales Skills
* Poor Communication Skills
* Easily Derailed by Fear
* Don't Consider the Human Aspects
* Lose Sight of the Owner's Investment

Now let's look at what successful agents do; how they think and how they stand out from the competition.

Chapter 2:
The Successful Agent

Successful Agents Cultivate Habits for Creating Success
Successful, top-producing agents who consistently close business tend to be quite progressive, early adopters of new technologies and winning strategies. They are constantly out there looking for new ways to improve their business. They don't necessarily try everything that is presented to them; instead they scrutinize and analyze new products, tools, methods and resources first.

They also stay the course and persist in their efforts even if it doesn't produce immediate results. While striving to always be improving on their business, they see their business as a real business. And just like most other businesses, some things take an investment of time, money and resources to see dramatic results.

Successful Agents Spend Time on Growing their Business Daily

The best agents are constantly adjusting their strategies over the course of their real estate career and they don't expect that things will happen right away. These agents are consistently spending 10-12 hours a day building their business.

Successful Agents Invest in Branding their Business

While a return on investment in branding may be hard to pin down, the need for a consistent branding message is critical to attracting prospects and picking up listings.

Successful agents have an introductory video of themselves to showcase their value, and then ensure that they have an up-to-date mobile responsive website.

Great agents invest the time and resources to ensure their brand is consistently displayed across all forms of social media—Facebook, Twitter, Google+, YouTube, etc. Across all platforms, their message clearly expresses their values and promotes their website by directing prospects back to their website where they offer something of value for free, in return for a name and email for follow up.

The best agents find ways to shape themselves to their marketing in a way where they become very much like their clientele. They understand the struggles of their clients and what is important to them and then they deliver solutions that fit perfectly.

Successful Agents Think BIG

Successful agents think big. They think they want to take on over 115 to 250 listings a year. They're not thinking, "Oh, I just want to do one a month." They're thinking big numbers—and all the top producers think this way.

Successful Agents Associate with Success

Successful agents associate with people who have a lot of success. It's often said that your income is the average of the 5 people you hang around with the most. If you want to make more money, you probably need to upgrade the 5 people you hang around with the most, income-wise.

Successful Agents Pursue Personal Development
A successful agent knows that to be effective they need to continually pursue personal development to gain new skills and learn new techniques to help give their business a competitive edge.

Successful Agents Invest in Their Business
Successful agents are careful to budget and invest money back into their business to help it grow. Successful agents invest a minimum of 10% of their annual income into improving themselves and their business.

Successful Agents are Great Communicators
Being an excellent communicator, they give clear answers to client questions that show they've done their homework. They go the extra mile for their clients by leveraging many types of resources to be able to provide service to their clients that is not just comparable to other agents, but that blows other agents out of the water. Simply put, they operate on a higher level playing field.

Successful Agents are Planners
The successful agent plans and is organized. They have a business plan.

Successful Agents have Coaches
They have a coach. They actually have 2 kinds of coaches. One is a coach for them personally on their performance, and the other is a coach for their business, who specializes in their industry and can help them put the right systems, resources, plans and strategies in place.

Successful Agents go to Seminars
They go to 3 or 4 seminars a year. They work with people who are better than them.

Successful Agents have Mentors
They have mentors. They pay their dues (more about paying dues later).

Successful Agents Give Back
Experienced, successful agents help the new agents. They give their time and money to charities and philanthropic activities.

Successful Agents Are Eager and Easy Buyers
People who sell great are great buyers. You will attract people who buy the way you buy. The most successful agents are easily sold because they want to attract easy buyers and be people who can easily sell.

Successful Agents Habits for Creating Success are:

* Put in 10 to 12 Hours a Day
* Invest in Themselves and in Their Business
* Think BIG
* Associate with Success
* Pursue Personal Development
* Budget and Invest Money Back into Their Business
* Are Great Communicators
* Are Planners
* Have a Coach (or Coaches)
* Go to Seminars
* Have Mentors
* Give Back to Their Community and Industry
* Are Eager and Easy Buyers

New agents have additional challenges and a larger learning curve to overcome when they are just starting out. In addition to cultivating all of the habits of the successful agent, they also need to learn the industry and gain skills. We offer additional success tips for new agents in the next chapter.

Chapter 3:
New Agent Success Tips

First—New Agents Need to Find Help

When you're a new agent starting out, you want to start with an office that's going to give you training. We can't emphasize enough that when you are a new agent is not the time to go it alone, you need to learn from those with experience in the industry and from successful leaders and teams. This alone will shave years off of your learning curve and help your business become successful much faster.

Yes, you'll probably have to pay more on your split with the broker, going at a 50-50 or even 60-40, and in the right office it will be worth it. The broker is due more because of the time and energy they're investing in you, and you're "Paying" for your education through the bigger split you're giving the broker.

New Agents Need to Partner with Success

As Anthony Robbins says, "Proximity is power." You want to get in proximity to the people who have what you want. You want to get close to people who produce the way you want to produce, so you can get the training, and more importantly, the habits, skills and mindsets they have. Being close to them will allow their way of doing business to become your new normal.

New Agents Seeking Success Should Work with a Mentor

In this context, a mentor is an experienced professional who agrees to train, council and guide you in your development as an agent. Find someone you respect, who has produced what you want to produce, and ask them to mentor you.

While we want you to find a mentor, we want you to take personal accountability to continuing to develop and educate yourself. Don't rely on your mentor for all your learning; continue to read books and attend seminars, masterminds etc.

New Agents Seeking Success Should Seek Personal Development Training and Industry Specific Training

There are 2 kinds of training new agents need. One is personal development for them to become more effective in life; the second is industry specific training. One doesn't work without the other.

Upgrading your business systems without upgrading yourself would be like buying a race car and not learning how to drive it. Upgrading yourself without upgrading your business would be like learning to drive a race car, yet never getting in one.

New Agents Seeking Success Need Industry Specific Sales, Marketing & Communication Training

New agents should make sure to get industry specific training in things like:

> *** How to Prospect**
> *** How to Sell**
> *** How to Marketing Yourself**
> *** How to Talk to Agents**
> *** How to Talk to Buyers**
> *** How to Talk to Sellers**

Observe and Emulate Success Stories
A close associate of ours is a great example of what effective agents do. Christian Fuentes co-owns Re/Max Top Producers in Diamond Bar, California. Christian has become Re/Max Diamond Award winning Team Leader, leading the Dream Team, a 10 member group that ranked No. 2 among Re/Max teams in California/Hawaii in 2012 and 2013.

Christian started his career in real estate with a job as an assistant. He knew it was important to keep improving so he started going to classes on how to be a better assistant. There he talked to people and found out what they did. He met some people that he felt were really fantastic so, using the idea of **partnering with success**, and recognizing the value of **mentorship,** he got a job with them and trained with them as a buyer's agent.

This whole time, he kept **personal accountability** for his development, taking seminars; training and development on sales, training and development on personal growth. He also was going to **industry specific sales, marketing & communication training** about exactly what to do as a real estate agent. He attended **Personal Development** seminars to make him a more effective and capable person.

Christian's hard work and determination has paid off in a big way. He continues to personally sell, earning his way into the Diamond Club the last 2 years! He recently ranked No. 10 on the National Association of Hispanic Real Estate Professionals annual list of the Top 250 Latino Real Estate Agent in America in 2013.

New Agents Should:

* **Find Help**
* **Partner with Success**
* **Work with a Mentor**
* **Seek Personal Development Training**
* **Get Industry Training in Sales, Marketing & Communication**
* **Observe and Emulate Success Stories**

There are specific personality traits, in addition to training, experience and personal development that are shared by successful agents. The most important of these traits can be taught and cultivated. Successful agents know how to sell, how to effectively communicate and they have also worked on their subconscious programming to eliminate their internal set of limiting beliefs. In the next chapter, we will explore how you can learn from their success strategies and apply them to your own business.

Chapter 4:
Traits Of The Successful Agent

Know How to Sell and Communicate

Successful agents have several personality traits in common. The number one success trait of successful agents is that they know how to sell and communicate. That doesn't mean they are pushy or too 'salesy'; just the opposite. The top sales people are truly servants. They know the sales process depends on being a great communicator, finding out what their client wants and helping them get it. That's where successful agents shine; they know how to effectively communicate in ways that their clients understand.

Work on Subconscious Programming to Eliminate Limiting Beliefs

If you gave an agent a perfect marketing plan, but she didn't believe it would work, she wouldn't use it. If a home seller was ready to list, but the agent didn't believe it he wouldn't ask for the listing. If you think you're only worth a certain amount of money, you won't allow yourself to make more than that amount, or you'll sabotage and lose the money.

Limiting beliefs can stop you from applying systems that work, growing your business, and having the income and relationships you want.

To overcome the prison of limiting beliefs, all truly successful agents have worked on their subconscious programming. They've eliminated self-defeating thoughts and ideas from their mind and heart and have reprogrammed themselves with patterns that lead to success.

Have a Positive Attitude and Mindset

Successful agents and successful people are positive, have an incredible attitude towards business and life, are passionate, and love what they do, and they're willing. Willing means they're willing to go to work, they're willing to try something new, they're willing to have a conversation, they're willing to pick up the phone, and they're willing to do whatever it takes. The proper mindset for success is one of the most powerful tools in the successful agent's arsenal.

Have the Capacity to Keep Moving Forward with Determination

The third trait is they have the capacity to keep moving forward. Life is going to happen. Babies are going to be born, people are going to get sick, things go wrong, fear will come up, and lack of money will come up. Things like the economy changing come up, things like 9/11 come up, but effective and successful agents have the capacity to move forward despite obstacles.

We know people who made more money between the terrorist attacks of 9/11 and the rest of the year than they made the previous 9 months because they didn't quit. They kept moving forward. While other agents quit, they kept going and had the market to themselves.

We see this today: there is so much discouragement in the world today, your competition is quitting or just going through the motions. If you're willing to go for it, full out, you'll make so much more because you'll be one of the only ones going for it, you'll have much less competition, and people will choose you for what you represent: the hope and energy called determination.

Know How to be Productive for Their Industry
The fourth trait of all successful agents is that they know how to be productive for their industry. They know what they need to do on a yearly down to a daily basis in order to be productive and effective. They're tracking their numbers, they are sourcing their business and they have a crystal clear understanding of where their business comes from. They understand market analysis and learn everything about their target neighborhood or their 'farm area.'

Market Themselves and Their Business
They are also great at marketing themselves and their business. This means that people in their area recognize their name, their business name, maybe even their photo and their business is associated with positive outcomes.

Personality Traits Shared by Successful Agents:

* **Knowing How to Sell**
* **Being an Excellent Communicator**
* **Working on Subconscious Programming**
* **Eliminating Limiting Beliefs**
* **Have a Positive Attitude and Mindset**
* **Capacity to Keep Moving Forward with Determination**
* **Being Productive for Their Industry**
* **Marketing Themselves and Their Business**

Sometimes becoming the #1 choice involves subtle traits that new agents might not recognize. In the next chapter we will take a closer look at the power of connecting with the "competition" and being helpful as unrecognized vehicles to draw success to you.

Chapter 5:
Become The #1 Choice

Be Easy to Work with

Really successful agents are easy to work with. As an agent, I knew which agents would be difficult to work with. The easy agents to work with would say things like, "Hey, don't worry about that inspection, we'll get through this thing together. We'll make it happen."

Here's how it plays out in real life: If I had an offer from 2 separate agents and I knew one of them was difficult and one of them was easy to work with, I would tell my client which was which. Think about it, if you're a home seller, do you want to deal with a buyer's agent who is going to nitpick and go for more than what's fair to the buyer, or an agent who, while respecting their fiduciary duty to the buyer, is going to work to make the deal fair and smooth? By the way, I think part of the agent's responsibility is to make the deal smooth - because if it's not, the deal could fall apart for poor reasons, and that's s not in anyone's best interest.

The ones who were easy to work with would get more of my deals because it was easy to work with them, and that meant the deal was more likely to close, which meant my client would be happier. My clients got what they wanted, the other party got what they wanted, and the agent made more commissions because they were easy to work with.

Be Helpful
The big thing that's unseen in the market, especially for new agents is the really successful agents do things for other people; they're helpful. They don't see the competition as competition. The most successful agents get that we're all in the same business but that there's more than enough business for all of us, and that the more people they help, the more success comes their way.

Reach Out and Connect with the "Competition"
They make friends with other agents. We've seen the successful agent host a happy hour and not only invite agents from their office, they'll invite agents from other offices to attend. Why do they do this? In my career as a real estate professional, if I'd had a drink with an agent before we sat across the negotiating table, we had rapport and the deal would go 100 times better. If we were friends we could deal with the negative home terminate/inspection/survey reports much easier and come to solutions where the buyer and seller won.

The successful agent is looking out for the wellbeing of others, and if someone has a problem, they'll reach out and help them.

Become the #1 Choice by:

* Being Easy to Work with
* Being Helpful
* Connecting with the "Competition"

There are many real estate agents they may work within the same geographic area or type of sales. New agents can find it hard at first to differentiate themselves from the other agents who may also work in their local area. In part, this is because they are still busy learning the industry and deciding which area of real estate they may eventually specialize in. In the next chapter we will look closely at the importance of learning to brand <u>yourself</u> and your business with some marketing tips and strategies.

SECTION 2: POSITIONING

Chapter 6: Marketing Yourself & Your Business

Grow the Pie

The biggest thing about marketing is that it's got to be consistently evolving the business. If you picture the business like a circle, we want it to constantly be growing the circle, making it bigger and bigger. Some people talk about available business with the metaphor of a pie, where there's only so much to go around and to make more you've got to get a bigger slice. While that's ok, we think there's a better way: we want you to be constantly growing the pie and getting a bigger piece of a constantly bigger pie. The truth is, if you're good in business, there's really no limit to the amount of available money and business; there is no fixed pie.

Fill the Funnel

How do you do that? Talk to new people. Effective agents are always talking to new people. Whether that talking is personally by making cold calls or knocking on doors, or they duplicate themselves and have buyers agents, listing agents or a team that knocks on doors, they put out ads to their farm area, or through their website and internet marketing, the successful agent is always talking to new people. It's all just different forms of talking to people. Even internet advertising is just a form of talking to new people.

Expanding Your Sphere of Influence

Successful agents are constantly making contact with new people and expanding their sphere of influence. Expanding your sphere of influence is like creating a virus but in a good way. A virus will multiply exponentially. They essentially make their message 'go viral,' reaching more and more prospects and then their prospect's contacts.

Because they're excellent communicators, they turn relationships with friends and family into referrals. One, they know how to ask for the sale, and two they make it known what they do in a way that's okay for their sphere of influence.

Don't join the NFL

While they are constantly expanding their sphere of influence, one thing successful agents are not is annoying. A lot of people don't like ineffective agents, for the same reason a lot of people don't like network marketers, it's because the agent joined the NFL. No, it's nothing to do with football; NFL stands for "No Friends Left." That means they're so annoying about pushing their business on everyone that nobody wants to talk to them.

For example, we were asking an agent friend of ours at lunch one day, "Would you give your business card to this server and try to do business?" He said, "No, probably not. I don't have a relationship with her. There's not been an expressed interest. Maybe if she was in my farm area I would, but I'm not just going to give my card or push my business on just anyone."

Remember Business is Relationship-Based

What effective agents understand is that this business is relationship-based and there's got to be a context for the sharing of the business card or the asking for the business.

So how does the effective agent get the referral without being annoying? They establish the relationship first and then out of the relationship comes the referral. What ineffective agents do is they push their business left and right, without thought for the relationship, and it just drives people away.

In the book, *7 Levels of Communication*, Michael Maher told a story about an agent named Michelle that took a unique approach that really paid off.

This is an excerpt from Michael Maher's book:

> *In a market that was down 40% in number of sales and 20% in sales price, we've INCREASED our business by 78% in transactions and our volume by 49%. Most of that came in the last six months.*
>
> *One of the most important factors in your homeownership experience is your relationship with your neighbors. Even in today's fast-paced world, we need to take the time to get to know the people around us. So now we throw a housewarming party for every one of our buyer-clients as a way to meet those neighbors. We throw them a party thirty to forty-five days after closing. That timeframe seemed to work best.*
>
> *We cater the food, put out branded signs and take a picture with our clients in front of the house with a sold*

sign. My coach also suggested that we give out door prizes so that each guest fills out a door prize entry form. That's how we get information for follow up and ask for referrals.

We get three or four referrals on the door prize entry forms at every party. It generally costs between 200 and 300 dollars for food, but I'm lucky enough to have several partners in my business who help me with the cost for the party.

I used to be really shy and I was still coming out of my shell when we did our first few parties. My coach suggested I put myself in the role of a server. As soon as I did that at the parties, not only did I feel more comfortable, but I got more referrals!

We used to wait until closing to ask the clients if they wanted to do a housewarming party. That didn't go over so well when they were stressed out about moving. So after some trial and error we got smarter and began explaining the housewarming party at the initial consultation instead of waiting until closing. We just made it a part of the process. You get pre-approved, make an offer, get a contract, sign papers at closing, then host a housewarming party.

Our system was pretty good four months ago. Then my coach showed me how to take the parties to the next level. First, he suggested that I call all invitees to confirm that they would be attending. We were sending nice invitations out and I felt that was enough. I figured it was up to the buy-client to get them there. But my coach kept emphasizing that we wanted to immerse ourselves in our buyer-clients' circle of friends.

To maximize my time, I needed to get as many as possible to that party. So I began calling to confirm and attendance soared. Instead of getting 50% or less, we are now getting more than 75%. And with more people, the energy is also higher. The clients seem to enjoy themselves more. These parties are a lot of fun!

Michelle's success is a great reminder that marketing is simply talking to new people, the importance of focusing on relationship first, and it also emphasizes the importance of having a coach to help guide you.

Next, we'll take a look at why personal coaching can also become a springboard for your success.

Chapter 7:
Coaching

Get a Personal Coach

We don't know a single successful real estate professional that hasn't been through a ton of coaching and seminars. The brokers and the top agents we work with are all constantly doing the important and smaller dollar things like reading a book or listening to a CD, but most of them are doing the bigger dollar things too, and they have a personal coach and they're going to 3 to 4 seminars a year.

Surround Yourself with High Achievers

Work with people who are better than you and surround yourself with high achievers. The top people make a difference in the lives of people who aren't as successful as them, they want to pass it on and yet they also insure their success by having a peer group of highly effective people. High achievers want to associate with high achievers - become one and spend time with them.

Pay Your Dues
Every successful agent has, at some time, paid the price. Paying the price means being an assistant and working contracts. Whether you're filling them out, doing all of the leg work and hard work like going to the open houses, door knocking or prospecting, it's all part of paying your dues. Paying the price (paying your dues) includes things like calling all the 'for sale by owner' listings, or calling all the expired listings.

Top agents have paid their dues and understand what it takes to get to the next level. As you grow, you'll develop a team that can do these important tasks, but until then you have to put in your time to get to that level.

Keys for Success:

* Get a Personal Coach
* Surround Yourself with High Achievers
* Pay Your Dues

In the next chapter, we'll look at the three things new agents on the path to success do consistently: knocking on doors, attending open houses and cold calling for sale by owners, open houses and expired listings. Paying your dues, pays off in the end with more sales and closings!

Chapter 8:
3 Successful Agent Daily Activities

3 things new agents on the path to success and super successful agents do to market themselves are:

* Knocking on doors
* Attending open houses
* Working the phone cold calling for sale by owners, open houses and expired listings

The Daily Regimen of the Successful Agent
What we see first and foremost when dealing with the top 7-10% of agents, like highly successful agent Christian Fuentes, is their self-discipline and their daily regimens.

Schedule Your Learning

Looking at their daily schedules, they set time aside each day to continually be investing in themselves and learning. Whether it's how to speak to people or just how to close more transactions, or learning more about financials, they are in a constant state of learning and self-improvement.

Get Enough Sleep
Successful agents know their day's success begins the night before when they go to sleep. What time you go to sleep will determine how good your day is today.

Keep it Positive - Go to Sleep the Right Way
Too many people go to sleep watching the news or watching something negative on TV and it programs their subconscious in a negative way; when they get up the next day, they're in a cranky mood, a bad mood and things go sideways for them.

The successful agent programs themselves with positive things the night before, so they wake up in a good mood, with positive expectations and things go well for them (they also go to sleep at a reasonable time and then get up early).

Exercise and Eat Healthy
Even though they have to work a long day, they find time to exercise. There's so much research out there showing that exercise releases endorphins and releases happiness chemicals, we don't even need to address it in this book. There's research showing that the right kind of exercise actually releases the chemicals that allow the brain to lay down the wiring to learn better.

Knowing they have a long day, they fuel and fill their body with good nutrients.

The body, the brain and the emotions have a connection. If the body goes south, the mind and the emotions will go south. If you train the body up, if you get more energy in the body, if you eat healthier food, your body will come up and that will bring your emotions up and that will bring your mind up, which results in a better you, a better business and more income.

Spend 35%-40% of Your Day with Past Clients or Prospecting

For 35% to 40% of the day, successful agents are keeping in touch with their past clients or prospecting. They also do a lot of door knocking for new clients. It's mandatory to door knock, and most of the successful agents do it themselves or they have a team member do it for them.

Start Your Day Between 7am and 8am

We see that they're showing up to work between 7 and 8am. That's their start time and they're working 10 to 12 hours a day consistently. Successful agents are self-disciplined and consistent every single day with their schedule.

Pay Attention to Your Attitude Each Day

Ultimately, they just have an incredible attitude towards business and life and they're very passionate about what they're doing. Again, they're constantly receiving training and development on how to better themselves and their inner programming.

The Daily Regimen of the Successful Agent:

* **Keep a Daily Schedule**
* **Get Enough Sleep**
* **Keep TV/Media Consumption Positive**
* **Eat Healthy and Exercise**
* **Focus on Nutrients to Increase Your Learning Power**
* **Spend 35%-40% of Your Day with Past Clients or Prospecting**
* **Start Your Day Between 7am and 8am**
* **Pay Attention to Your Attitude**

Now that you understand the 3 daily activities that successful agents are sure to do and you see the daily regimen of success agents, we'll take some time to explore the three types of income you need to focus on. It's not what you think: money isn't the only ingredient for success.

Chapter 9:
3 Types Of Income

There are 3 major types of income we get from any job. One is emotional, one is mental, and one is financial.

Emotional Income
Emotional income is how the job makes you feel. A lot of artists, for example, feel great creating their art. They feel amazing when someone buys their art, but maybe they don't make a lot of money until they become well known. They get huge emotional rewards. A lot of teachers get motivated by teaching because there are huge emotional rewards in that industry.

Financial Income
Many people get into business for financial rewards and that's where you make a lot of money. Most people, unfortunately, base their choice in industry, their choice of profession, their

choice of what they do and who they work for on finances...who's going to pay them most immediately.

Mental Income
The third kind of income is mental. That's where you learn how to do something. Think of the old days where a young person would learn a vocation as an apprentice, they work for cheap for the "Income" of knowledge.

The Mental, Financial, Emotional Income Tradeoff
When I wanted to get into the seminar business, I identified the person I wanted to learn from, and I said to myself, "I'm going to start working for this guy." I moved from Orlando to Las Vegas, where he was, with no promise of a job, and I lived on a friend's couch. I was still was paying the mortgage on my home in Orlando and I worked for this guy pretty much for free; I would make money when I made him extra money.

I didn't make a lot of financial income, but I made a lot of mental income. I learned how to do the business, I learned what it took to grow a business, I learned how to change lives.

I had a lot of emotional income as I helped a lot of people. That feeling, of making a difference in someone's life is priceless, and I wouldn't trade it for any amount of money. To me, if there's not emotional income in it, it's not worth it. Some people make career decisions only on the financial income, forget about the emotional income, trade their happiness for a paycheck and become part of the story of soul-crushing jobs.

Because I was willing to sacrifice the financial income to get the mental income, I learned how to create huge financial income down the road.

That's the piece so many people are missing. They want the financial income right away but really they need to sacrifice and work for the mental and emotional income by first working for the best people they can find. They need to get as much mental income as they can, and then that will teach them how to increase their financial income. They say if you empty your pockets and your mind, your mind will always fill your pockets.

If you are willing to do for 2 years what no one else is willing to do; you can do what no one else can do the rest of your life.

The Power in Changing your Internal Beliefs

When I started going to these different seminars, it began changing my internal beliefs. I started going to every sales seminar I could. I'd get an email, I had no idea who the speaker was but it fit in my schedule so, I'd go to the seminar. I even took seminars on business etiquette, like how to eat at a business dinner.
I went to everything I could because I knew that my business was dependent upon me: the more I improved myself, the better I'd be, and the better I'd be the better my business would be.

Now that you understand that there are three different types of income (emotional, financial and mental) and that each type is equally important to your ultimate success, we will explore another key skill, that of learning to be a good, clear communicator.

Chapter 10:
Communication Is Key

The most important place we can improve ourselves is through our communication. Because our communication is both internal and external, everything we have in our life is created through it.

Our internal communication dictates what we will and won't do. If we want to get ourselves to do something, we'll either do it or not do it because of our internal communication. If we want to get ourselves eat a certain way, to make a marketing call, to exercise, whatever it is, we're either going to talk ourselves into it or talk ourselves out of it.

Don't Kill the Deal!

Our external communication drives what we can inspire, or fail to inspire, others to do. If we want to get a sale, contract or a better price in negotiation, we'll either get it, or not, because of our communication.

When we're working with our prospects and clients, our communication with them will either talk them into or talk them out of the actions that cause progress in our business - it will either facilitate or kill deals.

For most agents, their lack of training is killing deals. It's not that they need to learn so much more about how to do real estate, it's that they have got to stop killing deals by saying the wrong things and being ineffective in their communication.

Everybody Can Learn to be an Effective Communicator

The good news is that everybody can learn to be an effective communicator. Absolutely everybody. There are many products and workshops out there to help. Jase offers a complete communication system to help agents learn the skills of communication so they can make more deals.

For example here's one communication skills every agent must know in order to close more deals:

How to read body language

Not knowing body language can kill your deals

If someone does not know how to read body language, they'll probably close too early or close too late and lose the deal. It's like a guy on a date. If a guy doesn't know how to read the signs and he goes for the kiss too early, he's lost the date, and he gets slapped. If he goes for the kiss too late, he's lost the date.

As a real estate professional, if you close too early, and your client is not ready, they'll balk and leave. Close too late and their interest wanes and they walk. You got to know the buying signals; you've got to know how to tell when to close.

Here's some simple buying signals (see Jase's product for a more in depth study):
*An emotional shift
*The buyer has a shift in volume and gets quiet or loud
* They "Touch" or "fondle" the house in a soft, loving way
*The client asks questions about the property (except for "Planner" personality types who ask questions about almost everything)
*They pick up the contract to read it and get a better look
*They're mentally placing furniture

Sales on the Road from Contract to Close...
It's one thing to get a client, it's another thing to get the client to sign a contract, but it's quite another to get it to close. A real estate transaction is not like a sprint. It's more like running the hurdles. There's going to be a ton of hurdles in the transaction...there's going to be obstacles.

There's so much work and hand-holding and emotion management that goes into the time between getting the contract signed and closing the deal. If people don't know sales skills, they're going to fail. It's one thing to make the "Sale" and get the contract signed, and where your biggest selling will come in is in keeping the client in the transaction, stop them from bailing and get them to press through the obstacles.

Getting a contract through to closing is a constant process of "Selling."

Learning to be a good communicator is an important skill, but you also need to know, understand and live the 4 components of sales: Marketing, Conversion, Delivery and Referral. This is a cycle, and the cycle is what drives the success of your business. Fail in any one component of the 4 components of sales and your business will not be able to truly thrive. In the next chapter we will discuss each of the 4 components of sales in detail.

Chapter 11:
4 Components Of Sales

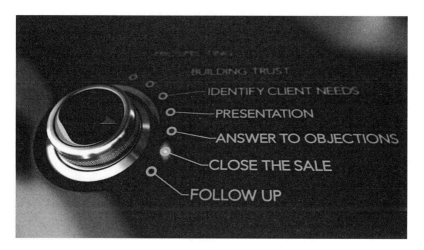

Communication and the 4 Stages of Any Business:
There's an easy way to understand how important sales skills are by thinking about the four stages of any successful business.

Marketing
The first part is when a business lets people know that they're in business, and what they have to offer. That's called marketing, and it can take on many different forms: ads in the newspaper, on TV, blogs, social media, and invitations to events, to name a few.

Marketing let's people know you exist, it does not make money by itself.

Conversion
Once you let people know who you are and that you can help them, that doesn't mean they're a client yet. Now you've got to

do the most important thing for your business: sell them and convert them into being a client.

Cash is the life-blood of a business. When the company has no "Cash" (whether in paper currency or available in an account) the company dies. Cash comes from "Sales" either selling a product or service, or selling someone on making the business a loan. Either way, ultimately the business needs to make sales and generate cash or the business is out of business.

In step 2, Conversion, you're doing the most important thing to keep your business alive: generate sales and thereby cash.

Delivery
This mean delivering on your product or service.
How well you deliver, or not, determines how happy your client is, and how much they'll want to talk about you. This is where you earn the referral, repeat, or upsell.

Referral, Repeat or UpSell
Step 4 is asking for the referral, repeat or upsell.
It's also providing ways that your client can make referrals, repeat, or upsells for you

So, What Makes an Agent Succeed or Fail in Each Stage?

Stage 1 Marketing: What is marketing but a, usually outbound, conversation about your business? What makes a conversation go well? Communication skills.

Stage 2 Conversion: This is where you sell. What makes sales go well? Communication skills.

Stage 3 Deliver: What makes delivery go well? Out of all four stages, this one is most dependent on your performance, ie, being on time, being excellent, delivering as promised, good quality, good price etc. What can impact it, to make you most effective? Knowing what the client wants and helping them get it. How do you do that? Communication skills.

Stage 4 Referral, Repeat, Upsell

To even have hope for a referral, a repeat client or to make an upsell, you've got to do well in Stage 3. Assuming you've done well, the client won't automatically know to refer you, or they won't know how. They also won't automatically buy from you again or buy more from you.

How do you get your clients to refer you, buy from you again and buy more? Communication skills.

Your Capacity to Communicate Drives The Sales Process

Ultimately, what makes marketing work or not work is your capacity to communicate. What makes them either become a client or not, is your capacity to communicate.

Step 3 & 4 are Where You "Do" Your Business

Step 3 and 4 is where you actually do your business and then whether or not you get a referral. People often think if they do great in step 3, "Oh, I'm a great real estate agent and I helped them buy this fantastic house," they think they're just automatically going to get the referrals but that's not true.

Whether or not you get a referral comes from how you ask for the referral; the way you structure your business to automatically get the referrals, the way you have conversations all along the way to get the referrals or the repeat business. That's driven by communication.

75% of Your Success Comes Down to Your Capacity to Communicate

Out of the 4 major parts of the sales process, 75-100% of it comes down to your capacity to communicate. People wonder why people go out of business or they're not making as much money as they could, well it's because 75-100% of their business is predicated on sales and communication and they haven't studied how to sell or effectively communicate...and so they fail.

Think About the Client's Experience

Even though step 3 is based on delivering what you do, how a client perceived the experience of the real estate transaction, if they enjoyed or not, if they stay in the deal or they bail out, is based on how well or poorly the agent communicates. Even step 3 comes down to communication.

It's NOT the "Best" Person That Gets the Job...

You could say 100% of business is based on your capacity to communicate yourself. It's not the best person that gets the job. It's the one who sells best, it's the one who markets best, it's the one who communicates best.

How do people do it?

There are workshops, there's seminars, there's books, there's CDs. If there's any one thing we would recommend people invest the majority of their budget of time and money in, it's learning to communicate. Learning to communicate with themselves and with the outside world.

There's tons of sales training out there on these techniques and we even offer courses. Being a more effective communicator not only helps in business life but in life outside of business too.

Developing Relationships

When they're working with a buyer, the successful agent will develop the relationship in such a way that they will intentionally ask for referrals at the appropriate times and in the appropriate way so the buyer wants to refer them.

For example, delivering more than you're asked for and being professional are a big part of getting a referral. What makes it work is asking for the referral at the right time, which is right after you've over-delivered, and the client has noticed and appreciated it (how did they notice it? You use communication skills in the appropriate way to bring it to the attention of your client).

Some Marketing Ideas
Knock on Doors
Most agents just door knock to get a listing. Successful agents have their team door knock houses around the area after a listing sells, to let the neighbors know the house sold, and thereby pick up other people interested in selling.

Throw a Party
As a housewarming gift to the client, throw him a party. Make sure to personally invite that person's family, sphere of influence and the neighbors.

At the party avoid overtly, "Selling yourself". Use it as an opportunity to grow relationships. The most successful agents have had the training on personal development and because they're positive and know how to communicate with people, they're so likable and they're such a great person to just meet.

When they meet their client's friends and family, the agent naturally develops new relationships with those people and they'll either get business with those people or they'll get referrals from them.

Chapter 12:
The Power Of Pre-Positioning

Let's talk about making sales as an agent really easy. You've heard that people work with people they know and trust. How would it be for your business and life if you could have prospects know, trust and like you before you even meet in person?

A couple years ago, I had something really interesting happen that showed me the value of what I call pre-positioning. I had a client named Michelle, who made a friend named Kate and thought Kate and I would like to meet and discuss business as we're in the same field. Michelle said, "You've got to meet Kate, she's a trainer, too. She's really fantastic. You guys would get along great and maybe do some business together."

Kate and I talked briefly on a Tuesday and we made plans to meet for coffee on Thursday morning.

When we met for coffee, Kate was really warm. She was wonderful, she was kind, and she was warm. But she was *too* kind and warm. She was acting like she knew me; nothing romantic, but super friendly, really open to working together. It was like a foregone conclusion: we're going to work together somehow. I had never had a meeting like this. Finally, I stopped the meeting and I said, "I've got to ask you, this is different for me. What's going on here? It's just different; it's so warm so fast."

Potential Clients Should Already Feel Like They Know You
Then she said words that would change my life. She said, and I can still hear the words echo in my head "I Googled you. I read your stuff and I watched your videos and I feel like I know you already."

When I left the meeting, I thought, "Wow, that was really cool that she already knew me, trusted me, and loved me," before we'd ever met. I thought, "I'd like that to happen again!"

Then I thought, "Wait, *what did I do that made that dynamic happen?*"

I unplugged from my business for a couple days and I brainstormed. I thought, "What did I do?" I wrote out everything I had done up to that point to create that experience for our meeting. From that I created a system and started teaching the process in a live seminar. Then I distilled that down into a two DVD training called IN DEMAND: Marketing 2.0. The 2.0 represents the two way communication of the marketing on the internet today.

Generally, I'm not great at teaching people how to build clients out of the blue, what I am great at is how to position yourself so that your prospect chooses you instead of your competition. Or, if they're even considering working with you, they get a feel for who you are so it's easy for them to say yes to working with you.

Some Key Concepts from IN DEMAND: Marketing 2.0
Sales Don't Start at the First Meeting
It was so warm and so different at that first meeting that I was blown away. I was like, "What's going on?" Then I realized that while most people think the sales process starts when you meet face-to-face, what I got really present on and clear on is that whole sales process starts way before you meet in person.

The sales process really starts the moment they come in contact with your brand, your identity, or the thought of working with you.

For me, the first sale with Kate started when Michelle mentioned me to Kate. When my past clients, friends, or referral partners mentions me, that starts the sales process, and the way they mention me helps or inhibits the sales process.

Your Marketing Starts Selling Long Before You Meet
The next most important moment is when your prospect Googles you. After they are referred to you, see your ad or come across you another way, your prospect will start investigating you, and the number one tool they use is Google.

When someone Googles you, what comes up will starts or inhibit your capacity to make a sale later.

Do you even come up?
Does someone else come up?
Are there videos of you?
Are there media spots of you, on TV, Radio or Podcasts?
Are there video testimonials for you?
Is there social media on you?
Are there 3rd party review sites on you, like Yelp?
Is there a blog by you?

Do you have a social media presence?

When potential clients have videos to see, or don't, it starts the sales process and either aids or inhibits your capacity to make the sale.

How to make it easy and aid the sales process
Start forming that relationship long before the first face-to-face meeting. Put up videos of you talking and sharing yourself, videos of you talking about a property, testimonial videos from past clients and prospects, videos that you've cut that are just informal and fun, articles and blogs that talk about who you are and what you believe.

Just a note—some of them can be professionally shot, and really well done. Make some of the other of you just holding your iPhone out and talking to the camera.

"Behind the Scenes" Video
For instance, today I was speaking in Moapa Valley Chamber of Commerce, which is right by the Valley of Fire. It's right between Las Vegas and a city called Mesquite, kind of in the middle of a desert, but there are really beautiful things to see around there.

As a part of my journey today, I took some pictures and videos and then talked about the Chamber of Commerce. I also took pictures and videos of me just touring around the Valley of Fire. I put those up on Facebook and other social media sites so that people will see them and say, "This guy's for real. He's speaking at the Chamber of Commerce." and they'll get to know me as a person, seeing the tourist stuff. None of it will be professionally shot, because the point of it is to show me as a real person: people get to know me for who I am.

Make Sure to Flood Social Media
During a recent training for real estate speakers and presenters, we had a professional shoot video of the event, but

then we also flooded Facebook and other social media with normal pictures of us, like when we went on the High Roller, that big Ferris wheel in Las Vegas. We put pictures up of me hanging out with my people who attended the seminar.

The power of the video and photos is to show people who are thinking about working with me, "This is a real guy; he actually likes hanging out with his people. More importantly, people that come to his stuff like hanging out with him."

How does this translate to an agent?
An agent would do really well to start putting up pictures of clients enjoying hanging out with the agent, having fun with clients and just being a normal human being with her clients. It's especially effective to show that you spend time with clients who have already closed, it shows that you're not just transaction oriented, you're relationship oriented.

Utilize the Power of the Internet
I went across country a couple years ago on a speaking tour, and we did 11,000 miles over 70 days. We rented an RV in Las Vegas, went to Texas and then continued east through Tennessee. The trip was beautiful....and the holding tanks were getting full.

Never having rented or used an RV before, I didn't know how to dump the tanks. None of us did. The guy at the RV rental place gave us about a four minute class on dumping the lavs when we rented the RV, but we had never hooked it up and we didn't even know how to make sure the hose was on right.

To say the least, I was nervous about it - I certainly didn't want that stuff from the holding tank getting all over me. My crew and I talked about it and we decided that we needed to stay at an RV park, where we can get help to dump the tanks and make sure we do it right.

Now we wondered, "Where should we stay, and who will actually help us?"

Let me set the situation as we faced it: we're in the middle of Tennessee, don't know anyone who lives within hundreds of miles, have no idea who to ask for help, we really need the right place to get this done, we have to make sure the business we use will be helpful and we need to find someone now.

What would we do? Who can help us? If only we knew someone to help. If only someone could tell us who to use.

In other words, we're looking for a referral, but we didn't know anyone. We're looking for word of mouth - but we don't know anyone.

We say to ourselves, let's look for social reviews. Let's Yelp it. We fire up Yelp, and find there's 1 RV park with no reviews ... just a phone number and the address for the RV park. The 2nd RV park has an average of 5 stars out of a possible 5, it's been reviewed about 10 times, there were many pictures of the beautiful grounds and people wrote about how nice the staff was and what a lovely stay they had.

If it was you and you need to take care of your RV and you know nothing about where to stay, which one would you pick: the one that has no information or the one that has pictures, descriptions and good reviews? It's an easy choice, right?

When someone's considering working with a real estate professional it's the same thing.

Do you just have a listing and it's just contact info, or have you been reviewed, on an independent review site, did people give you a ranking, are there pictures of you, are there pictures of you with clients and are there good reviews of you?

It takes the information about you from a figurative black and white outline to a full color picture or painting. It makes it really easy to choose the person who's been reviewed.

I find that Yelp works well. Yelp is either an amazing tool or a necessary evil, depending on how you want to look at it. If not Yelp, use other social reviews.

The Strongest Form of Marketing Ever Now Has a Digital Version

Throughout history, what has been the strongest advertising or marketing way ever? Word of mouth. All social reviews, Yelp, Amazon and others, all they are is digital word of mouth.

How I Learned the Power of Digital Word of Mouth

Here's where I learned the power of digital word of mouth. I was talking to a woman about being a keynote speaker at her event. The people that referred me to her had actually never seen me speak, and didn't know what kind of a speaker I was; it was a 3rd party company that had referred me to this woman. She said to me, "I hope we can get the contract together for you to come out because I know you're dynamic, I know you're funny, I know your presentations are engaging and people have a good time and learn a lot."

I'm thinking to myself, "How does she know this? She's never seen me speak before." I asked her, I said, "How do you know that?"

She replies, "A friend told me." Just then, she paused. She took this real long pause and then after a moment she says, "Wait a minute, I read it on Yelp."

What realized in that moment was that in her brain, reading it on Yelp was as if a friend told it to her face-to-face. What clicked in my head was that social reviews are so powerful because people perceive the review as if a peer or friend is giving them a direct word of mouth endorsement.

So why not just put testimonials on your website?

There could be ways to manipulate the testimonials embedded on your website. Yes, typed testimonials on your website are somewhat effective, and you need to do them. The challenge with typed testimonials on your website is that in your prospects' eyes they could have easily been faked by the agent, or their web professional could have slapped it up.

The power of the independent review site is that it's independently reviewed. The people reviewing are real people. You can even email the reviewer directly and ask them about their experience. You can see what else they've reviewed, who their friends are, and even their picture. They're real. It's independent. It adds weight.

There could be ways to manipulate Yelp and put up false reviews, but that's not a smart nor ethical way to build your business and it would come back to bite you in the end.

Agents would do well to get a listing on each of the major sites and encourage and invite people to review them. Don't ever bribe someone for a good listing because that's just not ethical. I think it's okay to say, "If you liked my service, will you please review me?" It's not ok to say, "If you give me 5 stars I'll give you X."

It's fairly easy to tell if a review is fake. If a business owner has one good review and the person who did the review has no friends and only has done 1 review, chances are it's a fake review. If, on the other hand, they've been slammed, and the person who slammed them has only done 1 review that's probably fake as well.

Social reviews are powerful when added to your own website. You can screen cap the social review, embed a viewer that shows the social reviews live on your page, or link to them.

Chapter 13:
The Power Of Video

The Most Powerful Digital Endorsement Today is Video. Videos let the prospect see the reviewer and are effective because they convey emotion, are more interesting to the average person than text, ranks up faster in searches and today people have been conditioned to watch video. Video also says that you're up with the times.

How to Ask for a Video Review

You want to make it as easy as possible for your clients to refer you and you want to ask at the right time. When you do a good job, they'll love you and they love you most right when they sign the contract for the house and at the closing table.

When you're at a point where they're really happy with you, make it easy for them to endorse you. Pull out your camera and say, "Hey you guys as my service helpful to you?"
They'll say, "Yes."
Follow up with "Do you think other people will benefit by this?" "Yes."
"Do you think there's people who offer similar services that are nowhere near as good as me, or that don't care as much and won't be good for other people?"
"Yes."
"Do you want to help people choose someone like me so they get a better service?"
"Yes."
"Awesome. Would you help me out and help them out? Can we cut a quick video?"

The more specific the video the better.
The more specific they can make the testimonial, the better. You want to collect videos from different niches, farm areas and types of buyers and sellers, so that when a prospect watches the video testimonial from your client they'll say to themselves, "That person is just like me!"

If you can get a collection of 5, 10, 20 people on video, even if it's just recorded on your iPhone it will help you close more deals, and make it easier, too.

Testimonial Format
You want your client to first and foremost be like-able, and they do that by having high energy, smiling and keeping it short and simple.

VIDEO TIP #1: You will have to tell your clients to smile before you start filming!

VIDEO TIP #2: If you press record and your client immediately talks there will be no space in the video for you or your editor to put in transitions or titles. Make sure your clients waits a count or two after you press record and then starts speaking.

Here's format we like to use:
Hi, I'm (name), and I was a (first time buyer/upsizing/downsizing) in (location/farm area/type of neighborhood i.e., golf community/seniors only community/school zone). My (goal or challenge) was (I didn't know what to do/where to look/how to afford it/I wanted to get the most out of my house/We needed to downsize/Wanted a bit more space). I worked with (your name) and he/she did (whatever amazing thing you did that stands out in their mind. Note: when I say amazing you may be thinking that it needs to be some Earth shattering service, when in reality, many times what you do in the normal course of business they'll find amazing. For example, a first time buyer actually finding a place to buy will find it amazing. Examples: Helped me find a dream home/Gave me comps/Priced it right for a quick sale/got top dollar/helped me stage it/helped our offer get accepted instead of our competition). It only took (time frame. Note: don't use if it was really long). If you're a (whatever the client identified themselves as: first time buyer/upsizing/downsizing) in (location/farm area/type of neighborhood i.e., golf community/seniors only community/school zone) make sure you use (your name again).

Before I go on, I can hear some of you saying, "Well, if they say they're a certain kind of client or in a certain neighborhood it will kill the chance of getting a different client or in a different neighborhood."

I hear you, and I get your concern, and I invite you to set aside that concern and consider this: I do sales training, and frankly, much of what I teach is perfect for anyone in direct sales, it's as relevant for real estate professionals as it is for stock brokers, or plumbers or insurance agents or loan officers or title agents. Would you have picked up this book, however, if it said,

"Secrets of Top Producing Accountants?" Probably not. You are reading this because it pertains to you, the real estate agent; the more precise the marketing the better. When you send a video of a first time buyer to a first time buyer you'll be really effective.

Now, suppose you only have one testimonial video of a client, a first time buyer, and they purchased in a neighborhood called Golden Pond, and you send that video to a prospect in Green Valley who is upsizing. Will it put off the prospect in Green Valley? Not at all. The fact you even have a video testimonial will go a long way. How many of your competitors even have one video testimonial? The testimonials are related to your service as a professional and will help you get the client.

Imagine what it will be like as you build your inventory of testimonial videos and eventually you have so many that the next time you have a prospect in Green Valley upsizing you can send them a video of our last Green Valley upsizing client. How effective will that be?

When you have a really great client
If you have a really great client who is willing to cut you multiple videos, have them niche the videos by cutting one for the geographic area where they bought or sold and the second video, have them cut it for the type of client.

Someone downsizing would cut the first video to include the area: "I'm Tom and I wanted to sell my home in Willowbrook Estates and if you're selling a home in Willowbrook Estates..." In the second they'd talk about the type of client:
"I'm Tom and my family is growing, so my wife and I needed to sell our current place and get more space. Mary helped me sell my home and make enough to buy our dream home. If you're stepping up, and want to get top dollar on selling and the best you can buying, call Mary.

To reiterate, some video is better than none, and more videos, more precise, is better!

Testimonial Examples

Hi, I'm Jane and I just bought my first home! It's in Green Valley and I'm so excited! As a first time buyer I didn't know if I could really afford a home. I worked with Mary and she made what could have been a really confusing and hard process easy by introducing us to her team of lenders and inspectors, and helped me get my ideal home in my budget! It only took a few months from our first meeting to close. If you're a first-time buyer make sure you work with Mary!

Note: If you notice the template does not call for your client to mention your business. I'm risking getting some brokers mad at me, and this book is called Secrets of Top Producing Real Estate Agents, not Top Producing Brokers, so I'm sharing the real deal: as an agent you are growing your brand. When you're new you may have to leverage off the reputation of the Broker and Office, as you grow, however, you'll be growing your reputation, and frankly, one day you may leave, start your own office, or most likely start your own branded team within the brokerage. The time to build that reputation is now. If you're a broker already, have your own office, or have a branded team, then have then be sure to add that info into the testimonial.

Testimonial Example #2
In this example our agent has an established team.
Hi, I'm Steve and all our kids have moved out or gone to college, so we're downsizing. We're "Empty nesters," now and wanted to find a smaller place, but still have a nice place where we can have friends over. We worked with Mary. She helped us sell our old house in Golden Pond and find the ideal place in Green Valley. Mary helped us find the exact place. It's beautiful. It's elegant. It really makes a statement." If you're selling a house and downsizing, make sure you call Mary, with the Green Valley Brokerage Team, I'm so glad I did!

Upload Them to YouTube!

When you upload your videos to YouTube you'll be getting many simultaneous benefits:
- Your videos will be easy to see and share
- You'll be establishing credibility
- You'll be listed on one of the world's top search engines
- Your videos have a better chance to show up in searches than just normal posts. YouTube videos rank higher in the search rankings and do so faster than normal web pages.

Use YouTube Titles and Video Descriptions

For the title describe the type of client and area.
For example: "I sold my home in Golden Pond fast!"
"First time home buyer used Mary,"
"Executives stepping up, call Mary."

For each video, have a description that gives your contact info and describes the situation, area, type of client etc. and goes into detail. You could even just type out what your client said (you'll probably tighten it up a little).
For your contact info, I recommend you put your best phone number, email and all your links, including your website, Facebook page, Instagram, Yelp reviews, and other professional listings. As you consider what to put, keep in mind the context of the application of the videos: someone is considering working with you and they're checking you out - the more you can give them the better!

Make Lists to Track the Details and Easily Share the Videos

Make a list, like a spreadsheet or an Evernote or a Word document and put columns with info for each video:
1. Client name
2. What each video testimonial is about, first time home buyer, upsize, downsize listing, whatever it is.
3. Geographic Area
4. Direct link to the video.

Testimonial Videos

Client Name	Transaction Type	Area	Link
Jane	First Time Buyer	Green Valley	youtube.com/example1
Tom video #1	Listing	Willowbrook	youtube.com/example2
Tom video #2	Upsizing/growing family	Willowbrook	youtube.com/example3
Steve	Downsizing listing	Golden Pond	youtube.com/example4
Steve	Buying smaller	Green Valley	youtube.com/example5

When someone calls in to ask you about working with your service, what you'll say to them is, "Great, I'm looking forward to meeting you. I just helped someone out who was in your same situation. If I send you a 2 minute video will you watch it?"

Most people say yes.

Then you send them that video with the testimonial of a client who was in their position, or from that neighborhood, or if you have it, who was both.

Chapter 14:
Authority Marketing

Authority For Real Estate Professionals

*What exactly is this authority and authority positioning, and
why is it so important for real estate professionals?*

How Are You Positioned?

They used to say to just call yourself an expert until you are
one, or 'fake it until you make it'. But these days, the public is
savvy enough to know the difference and can instantly tell if
you're an authority or not.

If a prospect searches for you online and can't find anything
about you as a successful real estate professional, that's going
to throw up a red flag. Consider how you are positioned online
and in the media.

The Importance Of Being Seen As An Authority

Being seen as a credible, trustworthy expert expands your
reach, opens new doors of opportunity and invariably leads to
more deals and more success.

There have been a lot of agents that have come and gone over the years. The ones that are still in business year in and year out, that have longevity, are the ones that have positioned themselves as the credible expert in their field and invested in building their brand and image.

Dan Kennedy, arguably one of the most prolific marketing gurus has this to say about authority:

"The simple truth is, if you aren't deliberately, systematically, methodically — or rapidly and dramatically — establishing yourself as a celebrity, at least to your clientele and target market, you're asleep at the wheel, ignoring what is fueling the entire economy around you, neglecting development of a measurably valuable asset."

Get Inside The Mind of Your Prospects
Clearly buyer clients want to know that the agent they hire knows the local area, knows the neighborhood home values and the schools, etc. They want to make sure that they get the best value for what's likely going to be the biggest investment of their life.

Sellers want to know that the agent they hire will market their house so it sells quickly and for top dollar; and that the agent will deftly handle the challenges that come up during the sales process with expertise.

But it's more than that. They also want to know that you understand their problem; that you've helped other people successfully solve the same problem, and that you are able to help them do the same.

It's important as a real estate agent to position yourself in a way that prospects can easily make that jump and say, 'Yeah, they're the expert; they're the person I have to work with'.

The 4 Faces of Authority
In authority there are typically four different mindsets or methodologies; Joe Everyman, The Cowboy, The Wizard, and

The Soldier.

Joe Everyman

Joe Everyman has been there, he's struggled too, with maybe a short sale of his own for example. If a prospect is looking for someone to help with a short sale and they're talking to an agent that has experienced a short sale and really struggled with it and went through it and understands all the ins and outs of it now, and is featured now in the media as a short sale expert, and he's out there helping people with short sales, that's an Everyman. I've been there, I've struggled, I know what you're going through and I can help you. That's one mindset.

The Cowboy

Another mindset is the Cowboy. The Cowboy is someone that is no BS, doesn't hold back any punches, and tells you the way it is. A good example is Jillian Michaels, the personal fitness trainer on the television show *'The Biggest Loser'*. She doesn't pull any punches and she'll tell you if you're fat or you didn't work hard enough, she'll flat out tell you...and sometime she'll yell it.

That's another way of positioning yourself as an authority. Just telling people, 'Look, you need a short sale and the longer you wait the worse it's going to get so you need to get moving. You need to start taking action and these are the things that you need to do right now. Don't wait'. That's more of a Cowboy mentality.

Some of these mindsets may even be mixed with each other; each person has their own personality that these present to.

The Wizard

Another mindset is that of the Wizard. The Wizard is someone that has lots of experience, lots of information to be able to share and to fix problems. They know so much more than their prospects that they're seen as valuable because they have all this insider info into the industry and the prospects are able to tap into that by utilizing the Wizard.

Examples of the Wizard would be Tony Robbins, Oprah Winfrey, Steve Jobs.

The Wizard has specialized knowledge and powers to do things the average person can't do. This would be someone that's really well connected. We usually identify with the Wizard where they've gotten shortcuts to getting things done because they know what they're doing, they have insider information that the average person doesn't know about.

The Soldier

Finally, there's the Soldier mindset. The Soldier can be really effective, especially when it's really who you are. It's someone that has the knowledge and the willingness and the ability to make problems just go away. They're a defender. It's like, 'I've been there and I'm not going to let these things happen to you where I've seen them happen to other people'. They help to instill confidence. A lot of times they're perceived as the smartest person in the room.

You can think about experts like Dave Ramsey or Suze Orman. Any customer prospect who might feel overwhelmed or defenseless is the type of prospect that connects with the defender.

What is Authority Marketing For Real Estate Professionals?

Put simply, authority marketing gives agents the ability to educate and advocate for their clients and be recognized in their industry as a leader.

Manufacturing authority gives you a 'bigger voice' than other agents, resulting in a larger audience and access to a higher level clientele and bigger deals.

Authority marketing is like personal branding on steroids. Using many of the same strategies and tactics used by celebrity entrepreneurs and the sports and entertainment industry, there are many opportunities to position you as an authority in your industry or local area so that you become the number one choice when your prospects are comparing you to the average agent.

Authority marketing helps differentiate you from the sea of real estate professionals. Are you like all the rest of the agents out there? If so, people are blind to you.

Typical agents are a blur because they all offer the same thing, they're all saying the same things on their websites, but none of them are really educating their prospects, or providing really useful content, building relationships with them, letting them know that they can solve the prospect's problem and that they've helped other people with the same problem, and telling them what to do next. Those are the things successful agents do to stand above the crowd. So how do you do that with authority marketing?

It All Starts With Having An Authority Mindset
When positioning yourself as an authority, the first thing to do is to check your mindset and realize you're not trying to just brag and call yourself great.

You know more about the real estate industry and transactions than your clients do, right? And you're sincerely concerned and care about them and able and willing to help them aren't you?

If the answer is yes and you can genuinely look your prospect in the eye and say, 'I can help you', you are already an expert and an authority in their eyes. So embrace your own authority.

The most successful real estate professionals have an authority mindset. They have a plan for how they're positioning and presenting themselves that differentiates themselves from all the other agents in their local market.

In my best-selling book, "The Authority Mindset," I talk a lot about thinking like an authority. Most people aren't comfortable with just calling themselves an expert while putting themselves out there as an authority and saying, 'hey, look at me, I'm great, hire me.'

Often times I hear real estate professionals say, 'I don't want to be self-promoting or bragging.' Most agents aren't comfortable with that, but that's not what an authority mindset is.

Don't Mistake Arrogance vs. Authority

Arrogance is when you selfishly put yourself **ABOVE** others to benefit only yourself. *Authority* is when you find the courage to unselfishly **LAUNCH** yourself forward in order to serve others with your gift.

When you find that courage, you'll never have to call yourself the expert again because you will have become the person that others easily see as the expert.

So eliminate any idea you may have that authority positioning is about bragging. Shift your thinking from the mindset of needing to call yourself or convince others that you are the "Expert", which most people are extremely uncomfortable with, to the mindset of being an "Educator and Advocate" for the success of your clients, which most people can easily visualize themselves as and more importantly crave to be recognized as.

When you are able to communicate this to prospects, I promise it will be the most powerful tool you have.

What Does It Mean To Be An Authority

Clearly with all the competition, setting yourself apart is critical to your success. In any local market, there are hundreds of agents all competing for the same prospects that search the internet when deciding who work with.

Being an authority is about having third party credible sources quoting you as an expert in your industry. It's about being seen in various forms of media as an expert in a way that makes it easy for your prospects to see you as the authority you really are.

If a prospect looks you up online and sees you featured in the news, quoted in the media as an authority, stories of your successes and your involvement in the community and that you're a published bestselling author in your industry, you instantly become the number one choice when compared to the average agent...the authority people want to work with.

You Don't Have To Know It All

Often times when I meet with real estate professionals, they express some hesitation in calling themselves an 'expert'; expecting that someday the media will call them or that somehow after they've worked hard enough or long enough, someone will come to anoint them as an expert. But the fact is, you don't have to know everything there is to know about your industry to be seen as an authority.

Think about Dr. Phil. Dr. Phil is an expert. He's a psychologist, he has a television show and he's positioned as an expert. Dr. Phil doesn't know everything there is to know about psychology; he's not the best psychologist in the world, or therapist. He's positioned himself in such a way that he is seen as an authority. There are lots of examples of that type of expert positioning everywhere we look.

If you ask most agents, they all say, 'Yeah, I always look out for my clients, I'm always trying to do what's best for them'. If you're not featured in the media with that sort of information out there for your prospects to see, then you're the only one that knows it and that's not good for you.

Both buyers and sellers want to feel confident that the real estate professional they choose fully understands their situation. Whether it's a short sale/foreclosure, investor, boomerang buyer, for sale by owner...a key to breaking down barriers and establishing your authority is to demonstrate that you can help them and that you've helped lots of other people just like them.

For example, having press or a reporter quote you into an

article about the US economy and housing prices as a subject matter expert with other experts that gets published nationally automatically positions you as an expert.

Then leveraging that media attention into recognition through avenues and channels like social media, emails, a press page on your website, things like that - those are ways to, without bragging, position yourself as an authority and an expert that people want to work with.

The key here is that it becomes other people identifying you as an authority and expert go-to person in your field because you educate and advocate for your clients. Once you gain this recognition, you don't have to brag. You will have become the expert you really are in the eyes and minds of your prospects and clients.

How To Be Seen As An Authority: The Power of the Press
You want to be seen in the media regularly, be quoted in the media as an expert in your industry, along with other industry experts.

Being seen regularly in the media sends a powerful message to prospects. What's funny is with the media attention, comes more media attention.

Client testimonials are a powerful tool to building credibility; but having third party credible news sources quoting you as a subject matter expert in your field, along with other well known experts, can instantly build credibility even for a newer agent.

Typically when reporters are looking for someone to do a story with, they want to know that you've been in the media before; that you've done a story. If you're going to be on TV, for example, a reporter's going to want to see that you have been seen on TV before. If you have, they're more likely to call you because they already know you understand how it's going to work and that you're credible enough to be on television.

Make an effort to develop relationships with news reporters. Reporters are hungry for stories. Providing your expert analysis or unique insight in a well crafted news story is a great way to be picked up and featured in news publications or called on in the future to comment on industry news.

Check out http://www.helpareporter.com for ideas on getting yourself in the news.

You can also use media distribution services to put out press releases out about the things that you're doing that showcase your expertise and build your credibility.

This could be things like a public speaking event you are giving or a story about your community involvement. It doesn't need to be big huge events. It really can be that you're going to speak at the Chamber of Commerce or you're going to a monthly marketing group or getting a new accreditation, or you're going to be leading an educational seminar for prospects, or any of the little things that you're likely already doing, but aren't getting media attention for.

It's important to be seen in various forms of media as a subject matter expert or educator and client advocate. If you offer a seminar you're being seen as an educator, you're providing people real value and that's press worthy. Get that seen in the national press and then again leverage that attention into recognition through social media and through other channels that gets people to recognize you as an expert.

There's lots of ways to become an authority utilizing various forms of media. You can do your own podcast show, for example, and interview people in your industry. That positions you as an expert and with the technology that's available today, it's simple to do.

Another way to be seen as an authority is to be a contributor to CNN iReport. Providing non-salesy, informative and interesting content is a proven way to be featured on CNN and a great way to be seen as an expert when properly leveraged in social media channels. Who is featured on CNN? Experts are.

Think about creating your own magazine, a digital magazine, and offering other agents or other people in the real estate profession the opportunity to be contributors to that publication. Then, get the digital magazine out to your prospects and entire market. That's a great way to be seen as an expert in your industry and easier than ever with today's technology.

Perhaps one of the best ways of differentiating yourself is to become a published author.

Be Seen as an Educator and Advocate by Creating Micro-Specialized Books

In our society authors are seen as experts. Writing and publishing a book, or a series of books, is a great way to position yourself as an authority and to showcase your expertise as a credible expert.

Being a published author or having a best-selling book that solves the problem that your prospects have not only gains you instant credibility, it also makes people want to work with you, all things being equal, when compared to another agent. Keep in mind that a book does not have to be a 3 inch thick, 400 page complete guide to your field. It's a fact that people today are more likely to digest shorter more focused books that address a specific problem they have, so consider the concept of micro-specialization.

Micro-specialization is not trying to be everything to everybody. When someone's looking for something specific, a solution to a problem, the agent that solves that problem the best is the person that they're likely to use.

Most real estate professionals know the answers to the common questions their prospects ask. They know first time home buyers have a completely different set of questions for them than if they're working for an investor who flips properties.

When a client comes to you and you discover what their problem is, you can actually put the solution out in book form so you can say, 'Okay, here's the book for my investors', or 'Here's my bestselling book on luxury home buying in high end neighborhoods'. What if a prospect was searching online for an agent to work with and found your press release announcing your book about (fill in prospect's problem here) just hit the bestseller list on Amazon. Think that makes an impact? You bet it does.

Here's the power of it: Imagine a first time home buyer calling around for a real estate professional, but they don't know who to hire. Most of the agents attempt to book an appointment with them, but **none of them stand out.** Then, one agent says, "Can I send you a free copy of my best-selling Kindle book (or best-selling on Amazon book) about first time home buying?"

What would you think of that agent? Would they stand out? Who would you see first, the "Run of the mill," agent or the one who has a book? Who would you see as the expert?

The agent who is a published author will be seen an expert on the subject and will usually be given preferential treatment, be seen first and has an advantage in getting the client.

It carries so much more weight and you have so much more credibility as an agent when you're able to show a prospect that, 'Look, I understand your problem. I successfully help people with this problem. I have a best-selling book that shows that I help people about this problem. Lots of other people have been happy with me helping them and here's what you need to do next; here's how you can work with me'.

What's going through a prospect's mind: "I'm a first time home buyer and this agent has evidence of lots of other first time buyers that she's helped, and they all seem happy. She's also been featured as a fist time home buyer expert in media, and she's got press releases written about her as an agent for first time buyers. She's even got helpful videos about what to expect when buying our first home and she's providing me with valuable content that's helpful and useful. There are lots of examples of her understanding my problem 100%. She's micro-specialized one of the services she provides in a way that I understand and she's the agent I need to use because she knows exactly what I need.

Micro-specialization is really about targeting a very specific problem and identifying your solution and making that solution available to prospects in a way that is easy to understand. Your solution gives them exactly what they were looking for and features you as an expert because you know and understand what their problem is 100%.

After all, you've got the best-selling book, you're positioned as an expert and authority in your local market, you're seen by your peers and by other prospects and customers as an authority in that particular niche on that particular topic.

How to Leverage Your Book
• Send a copy, digital or printed
• Just make the client aware that you're published.

Even if it's just an icon on their website, or if it's an assistant answering the phone and they say, "You're going to be meeting with Mary about listing your home. Great. You know what? She just wrote a book that was a best-seller on Amazon about listing," you're going to be seen as an expert.

Another way to let it be known you're an expert is to say, "When I send you a confirmation email, how about I put a link in there and you can check out my book for free?" The funny thing is, that prospect might never, ever, click that link, but the simple fact that you have a book, sets you head and shoulders above your competition.
Carry your book in your car with you so that when you meet

with potential clients or you're out at an open house, they'll see that you solve the problem they have; suddenly they want to work with you.

Whether you give it away or just to have it there sitting on the counter when you're doing an open house, somebody's going to see your book and ask you about it. Better yet, if it fits their needs, give them a signed copy. Show them that you're signing it for them and give it to them; after all, it's the answer to the problem that they have.

Here's another great example of how to use a bestselling book for positioning. Imagine an agent gets up at a Chamber of Commerce meeting to give a ten minute presentation about a particular service they offer. He's talking to prospects from the standpoint of 'here's who I help with this problem and this is the benefits to using my service. (make it all about them)

Imagine the agent holding their bestselling book in one hand and pointing to the book with the other hand to emphasize certain points. Having a book is great but holding it up in front of an audience of people that are prospects and referencing material that you put in your book, your bestselling book ...

"For example, in my book in Chapter 4, I talk about how a first time home buyer can get the most value out of their home using three simple tricks", and pointing to the book as he's saying that, really carries a lot of weight into building his credibility.

When you hand a prospect your book, most are immediately impressed. The prospect might think, 'Wow, this agent gave me this book and if I go online I'd have to pay ten bucks for it'. It provides that instant feeling of value for them.

Instead of just a business card, an agent could have a whole series of one problem-one solution books that could be then handed to a prospect that has any specific need.

It's Human Nature
The nice thing is when someone gives you something that gives

you a feeling of value; you feel that they've valued you. When people value you, you want to do business with them.

People don't typically throw books away. As Americans, it's almost against our ideology to be throwing books in the garbage. Think about this...how many business cards have you had in the last year that have made their way into the circular file? Plenty, I'm sure.

A book is something different. It carries a different meaning behind it. It carries more weight and more authority.

You end up going from the mindset of 'where am I going to get my next commission' to 'what clients am I going to work with and help'.

What you're really doing is getting inside the mind of your prospects; showing them that you do understand them, that you have the answers, that you're qualified to help them with that problem and you understand the unique things about that particular situation.

The One Problem, One Solution Authority Book
By being the author of a short book that's squarely focused on overcoming just one of the most common obstacles faced by your perfect prospects, you not only create a valuable, credibility building asset that you can be proud of, you also establish yourself as an authority on a concrete topic that can attract media mention, speaking opportunities, radio, podcasts, TV interviews, opportunities that allow you to easily be recognized as the educator and the advocate; a person that's willing and able to help others.

Are you that person?

If you can look your prospects and customers in the eye, and confidently say, "I can help you," then you are that person.

Publishing an authority book is an opportunity to show others that you're that person.

You Don't Have To Be A Writer

Perhaps you have an idea for a book or you've even started writing one. Most of the population considers writing and publishing a book beyond their reach. This includes many, if not most, of your competitors. It's just not something they feel is achievable; so many get overwhelmed at just thinking about where to start. Maybe you feel that way too.

If you think you're not a writer, then you need to check this out, because it's very different than any book-writing system you've ever seen before, and you're about to understand why.

You see, after interviewing countless numbers of experts and entrepreneurs for books, articles, and guests on Business Innovators Radio, I've developed a formula that allows me to ask questions that automatically position my guest as the educators and advocates that they truly are, completely eliminating the subconscious needs and tendencies to be the expert and talk about themselves, but instead to speak with passion about the people that they help, and the solutions that they provide, effortlessly and without scripted answers. I know that this formula works; it's the strategy that makes the one problem, one solution book formula so unique.

Book Creation Process Outline

I start by creating an action plan. This is where we determine the best topic for the agent's book and define the reader, their perfect prospect. Then I guide the agent through a content discovery session. During the session, I record their answers to my questions and learn about their business, their passion, who they help and how they help their perfect prospects overcome obstacles, fears, misconceptions, and unknown pitfalls.

Once we've got this great content out of their brain, I show them how to organize it into the one problem, one solution book format template.

Then we create the perfect title for their one problem, one

solution book that will stand out in the short attention span market, and speak directly to their target audience.

I walk through the cover creation, editing, formatting, all the way to submitting their one problem, one solutions book to Amazon for publishing in both Kindle and physical format, so that in just a few weeks, they're holding their one problem, one solution book in the their hands, a book they can be proud of, a book that is truly valuable to others.

Keep in mind that creating a book is not about making money from royalties or even selling lots of books; it's about creating a book that sells YOU.

It's a Marathon, Not a Sprint
It's hard for some agents to understand that building authority is not a one shot thing that you do now, 'Oh yes, I got in the paper, they just had me featured so I'll have to wait six months or a year before they're willing to feature me again.' A lot of agents think, "well, I'm not doing anything really press worthy", but most really are.

Authority marketing doesn't happen with one article, it happens by consistently being featured in the media over a period of time, in various forms of media and being seen as an educator and advocate over the long term. Authority marketing never really stops.

The idea is that instead of being featured in one article every six months, successful agents might have a press release out every month or every two weeks. They're constantly seen in the media.

It's a different version of authority than most people may have grown up with. It used to be you'd put the newspaper article about you in a wood frame on the wall and now you're going to be featured in the media all the time.

Understand, the whole idea is to keep you in the news repeatedly. It doesn't happen overnight, it takes time to be known as an expert. It takes consistently being seen in various forms of media over a period of time, developing relationships with reporters and media contacts and a little 'tooting your own horn'. If you aren't singing your own praises, then who will?

Position yourself as the solution that solves your prospect's problems. You ultimately want more people to look at you as the number one choice when they're deciding who they want to help sell or find a new home.

Authority Image Marketing

Of course, all your marketing materials should convey your expert status and image. Image media marketing means your website looks professional and branded, like your business card, like your social media profile images and cover photos, like your promotional collateral –all your marketing pieces should have a uniform consistent and professional theme that's brands you as an authority. Be sure you have several professional headshots to use in various media publications.

Authority Marketing in a Nutshell

We've all heard the saying that "people do business with who they know, like and trust". Essentially, positioning all boils down to helping people get to know you, like you, and trust you. All things equal, if someone's not participating in authority marketing and they're not positioning themselves as an authority in their field or an expert or an educator of their clients and prospects and another person is, the expert is going to win out every single time.

What it boils down to is having the right mindset, discipline, and positioning yourself for success. You already care enough about your clients and their success. It's about positioning yourself in a way that people understand that; being seen in the media on a consistent basis, leveraging that through social media and other channels into recognition, and being seen as the credible source for solving customers' and prospects' problems with expertise.

The Benefits of Authority Marketing

* Increase revenue
* Increase visibility to past and current clients
* Increase listings
* Increase buyer clients
 * Increase referrals from real estate colleagues
* Be seen as a neighborhood real estate authority
* Improve the quality of your marketing
* Decrease time spent on your marketing
* Develop stronger image/branding of yourself
* Reach your potential clients more frequently
* Tap into new areas/markets
* Position yourself as an expert in a given category
* Be chosen by prospects more often

Position Yourself As Trustworthy With a Strong Online Presence

It used to be that if someone didn't know you in person they didn't trust your online identity. It's switched now and people won't trust you as a business professional unless have a valid and strong online identity.

Suppose someone has been referred to you, what's the first thing they're going to do to check you out? They're going to Google you.

If someone says they're a real estate professional, but when you Google their name and they are nowhere to be found, there is a sense of mistrust created...it may only be subtle but it can be enough to be passed over as the agent of choice.

While it's good to have a page on your Broker's site, if you don't have your own website, you risk being seen as a beginner, and it makes it hard to trust you as a qualified professional. A brand new real estate professional usually won't have the kind of internet presence I'm talking about. A professional has a large internet presence in place, which shows longevity to their profession and implies professionalism.

If you're an experienced agent make sure your internet presence shows it, and if you're new, you can appear experienced with the right internet presence.

Chapter 15:
Advertising & Buyers

Advertising Has Evolved.
It used to be a business would advertise their products or services and a potential buyer would see the ad and make a purchase. Maybe you've seen the old ad where the "Commercial" was woven into the TV show and the host would pitch the product and do the advertisements live. During a break they'd say, "I smoke Marlboro," or "When I'm going to use soap, I use this kind of soap."

Perhaps you remember the advertisement for Timex watches, where they'd put Timex watches on the blade of a propeller and they'd run the propeller in a tank of water. They'd pull it out and say, "It takes a licking, keeps on ticking" (if you haven't seen this or other old commercials, just search them on YouTube).

People believed in the ads and they trusted the pitchmen, so they bought the products. The advertiser would make more sales, and with the additional revenue buy more TV time, which would in turn allow them to sell more products, so they'd make more money, buy more TV time, sell more products etc.

This became what's called the TV industrial complex; really simple, really elegant, and very effective.

But advertising has changed, or more precisely, people have changed how they relate to advertising, which in turn has caused advertising to evolve.

The challenge today: how much do you trust ads today, and how much do you pay attention to them?

These days, we are bombarded by advertising; it's all over TV, magazines, the web, billboards and even the cell phone. Also, we've all been burned or have been lied to by an advertiser, so now people are more skeptical about ads.

In short, people have tuned out and turned off ads. If you think about it, when is the last time you actually *bought something off an ad?* Out of the millions of ads you've seen in the last year, how many made you go out and purchase the product or service advertised? Probably just a handful (we'll discuss those later). The other millions of ads just lost money.

Advertisements are even avoided when possible now. When you watch a video on YouTube do you typically watch the entire ad the runs before the video, or are you watching the countdown that says, "You can skip this ad in 5, 4, 3. 2 seconds." What happens as soon as it says you can skip this ad? Typically, you'll skip as fast as possible.

If you've recorded a show on your DVR do you watch the commercials or do you skip through them?

When "Typical" Ads Typically Work

If there's a product or service you need, and you're capable and ready to buy and there's an ad for what you need, the ad might be effective, especially if it has a "For sale" or a "Special price" headline. Even then, for most people, when they need something they'll go find it and research the best purchasing options.

How effective is it to run ads for the ready willing and able to buy? Let's begin to answer that by looking at what percentage of potential buyers fall into that category. Estimates say that about 3% of the buying population is ready, willing and able.

Fighting Over The 3%

That means that of all the people spending money on ads, they're fighting over 3% of the population. Sure there's money to be made here, but when you consider that millions of businesses are fighting over a measly 3% you may realize it's not a very effective way to go.

So, how does this show up for the real estate professional? You could say, real estate professionals who are holding open houses, are fighting and hoping to find that 3% that's ready, willing and able right now to buy. Ugh, slim odds.

Unfortunately, the news about advertising the old way just gets worse.

When you think about those ads on YouTube, how do you feel?

You're on YouTube, ready to watch a video, you click play and what comes up? Some ad. The ad is a distraction. It's an interruption. It's something that takes away from your quality of life.

Emotional State & Ads

We have three states: an emotional, mental and a physical state, and they play a huge role in ads.

If emotionally we're upset (or feeling any kind of negative emotion) and physically we look at something (even if it's unrelated to what we're upset about), on a subconscious level, we will mentally attach negative thoughts and feelings to the thing that we're looking at.

That means what we're looking at in the ad on YouTube can actually cause us to associate negative thoughts and emotions to it.

Back to our example of being excited to watch a YouTube video... up pops an ad, which interrupts us, delays our goal, and causes a momentary upset. While we're upset we're looking at the ad, which let's say is for a car. Unconsciously we'll attach that negative thought to the car being advertised, and we may even consciously mutter "Stupid ad," or, "I don't like that car anyway."

It's not a really effective sales model to upset the very people you want to sell. These video advertisers are pushing people away.

Don't Push Prospects Away

For a real estate professional, being like an ad can push away clients.

Let's take the example of a 'for sale by owner'. Yes, an agent can help a home owner sell their home, pay the commission and put more money in their pocket at the end of the day by using a real estate profession rather than selling by owner.

The challenge is not the service the professional can render, rather, the challenge is that the call to the owner can be an interruption and received like an ad. Also, with most agents fighting over the 3% that is ready willing and able, the home owner is flooded with calls.

Most real estate professionals, when they advertise, they're trying to catch that 3% that's ready, willing and able right now.

The Power of 67%
95% of businesses fight over the 3% that's ready, willing and able.

Instead of fighting over the 3% that's ready, willing and able, what if we could reach another 67% that's largely untapped. What would it do for your business to have 22 times more prospects and only a fraction of the competition?

The 67% I'm talking about comes from the following.

Willing and Able for the Right Deal
Roughly 7% of the market will buy (and when I say buy I mean purchase or list) if they get the right deal. They're not in a rush, but they're open.

One Day Soon
Another 30% knows that soon they're going to buy. For example their lease is up in 8 months and they want to move when the lease expires.

Didn't Know They Could
Another 30% of the market is in the dark: they don't know they are even qualified to buy, or that they're now in a position to sell.

The Other 30% is a no.
The last 30% is just a plain, "No," to buying or selling. Just accept it and move on, and if you're one of those agents who keep trying to talk disinterested people into buying, I

recommend you just quit that practice. Move on and focus on the 67%.

What if we could get that 67% of the market, while also marketing to the 3% that's ready now.

We could actually be reaching 70% in effective ways, and what we've got to figure out is how we structure our marketing in such a way to market the 67% of the market no one's talking to, and simultaneously pick up more of the 3%.

The beauty about the 67% is that usually no one is building a relationship with them, no one is marketing to them and not many people are talking to them.

That's why when those people get ready to buy, and join the 3%, real estate professionals are fighting for them at the last minute because no one's already built a relationship.

How to Build a Relationship Before the Other Agents
If we could provide value to their life, have an in personal relationship and help them learn about how to best buy or sell, have them research us and see our testimonials and that we're featured as an expert and authority in the media, and do it all ahead of time, who do you think they're going to go to when they're ready?

What we want to do is start putting structures and systems in place where people choose us because they get to know, love and trust us before they're ready to buy, before they've made the choice to buy or sell to that when they're ready they already have us: they have a relationship with us and they're ready to work with us.

The sale starts long before the first face-to-face interaction. The more you serve people before you ask for the sale, the more likely they're going to want to work with you.

Know the Adoption Curve – Who's Ready to Buy?

Many authors talk about the 'idea adoption curve'. As with any product or service coming to market, when someone's ready to buy or sell real estate, the way they go about deciding on what to do breaks down into five different categories.

The 5 Types Of Buyers

The 5 types of buyers are the innovators, early adopters, early majority, late majority and the laggers. The innovators want anything that's new and cool. The early adopters want a strategic advantage. Then there's the middle majority and late majority; think of them as Middle America. And finally, there are the laggers.

The Innovators

The innovators and early adopters, the innovators want whatever's new and cool, and they want it because it's new. Since they're purchasing something new, that hasn't been on the market long, they are people who are going to trust their gut or intuition. They need to be since new products don't have a lot of reviews or word of mouth.

Early Adopters

Early Adopters are looking for a strategic advantage - they are quick to buy and will do so in order to get some type of advantage. They're not the first to buy but they're fast because they're the type of people looking to improve their life quickly.

The Early Majority and Late Majority

The two largest population segments are the Early and Late Majority. It's very tempting to market directly to them only, and most ineffective marketers do just that.

The challenge with marketing only to them is that the Early and Late majority is a bit more cautious in the way they make decisions. As opposed to Innovators and Early Adopters, these people rely less on gut or intuition, instead, they look to other people, reviews and data to help them decide.

One of the key decision items for is they're looking to other people to tell them what to buy. They're looking for testimonials or referrals or from someone they trust. They want to purchase something with a track record and if you're marketing to them without having first marketed to the Innovators and Early Adopters you're going to find it rough going.

The Late Majority
The Late Majority is similar to the Early Majority, just even more cautious, and they won't buy until they see that a majority of the population has already purchased.

The Laggers
Then there are the laggers; those people take forever to buy and they waste your time. You want to identify laggers so you know who they are and you don't waste too much time talking to them. They'll just take up all your time and you'll never make the sale even if you spend all your time with laggers.

How to Get Sales: Get an Influencer on Your Side
The way to make sales is by working left to right in the bell curve of buyers. Get your sales first with the Innovators and Early Adopters, who are typically first to buy, and are very influential. Then, get the Innovators and Early adopters to get out the word of mouth about your business.

Typically they're already in positions of authority through blogs, speaking at meetings, running businesses and have direct person to person influence, so request that they help spread the work and you also want to put their testimonials all over social media, your website, YouTube and your other marketing.

What really is beautiful is when you market this way to 'leaders and influencers'; they'll do the rest of the marketing for you. You get that Christmas tree effect where your referral chart looks like a tree - you're marketing to the person at the top and then it branches out.

Find whoever is most influential in a neighborhood. If you're looking for listings, find the people who are decision makers and leaders in those neighborhoods and get them to talk about your product or service whether or not they've ever used you. Ask the influencers to mention you or post your services where neighbors share about what's going on in the neighborhood - like places where they can put up posting or announcement about community happenings, garage sales, and other notices.

Many of the influencers have blogs and Facebook groups and you'll do well to talk to them about the quality of your services and the virtue of your character.

How do you do that?

Make It About Them
Provide value of some sort. Instead of asking for sales and talking about yourself, flip your marketing so the entire focus of your marketing becomes, "How can I provide value to the people I'm marketing to so they'll either spread the word about me or when they're ready to buy they'll choose me?"

Create a mindset of service. The amount of success I have as a speaker depends on the attitude I have going in: if I go in with the attitude, "I'm going to sell this crowd, I'm going to sell like crazy," my sales will usually go very poorly.

On the other hand, if I go in with the attitude of, "I'm going to serve these people and their life will be better forever because they met me, because they had an interaction with me whether or not they ever purchase from me," I make more sales and my sales go through the roof.

Ways to Serve Your Community

Write articles for neighborhood blogs, put out free price comparisons, talk about what's been sold. Make sure that your mindset as you write is to be purely of service.

Create a Local Event
One of the real estate professionals I know puts on a pumpkin carving festival every October and the community loves it and her business grows. The community gets to have a fun, free event and she gets center stage.

She gets local businesses involved. Restaurants donate food and other businesses sponsor the event, thereby getting publicity for their business and absorbing the costs of buying the pumpkins and setting up the event.

All these businesses would get exposure. *But who's the lynch pin who put it all together and gets the most goodwill and exposure?* That one real estate professional; think of it, every conversation that she has about the event with every person that's involved, every company, every sponsor, every volunteer, it's a mini marketing message for her, and she doesn't even have to talk about what she does, - they know. That's an example of a beautiful, elegant way to create a win-win, give back to your community, and get exposure.

Throw a Seasonal Party
Throw wine and cheese parties in the winter, and neighborhood barbecues in the summer. Follow the example of the pumpkin party and get local businesses to sponsor and a restaurant to host.

Radio Shows
Whether you're a guest or producing your own show, being on the radio positions you as an expert.

You can pay to host your own radio show on AM, FM or Internet Radio, and record the radio show live and rebroadcast it as a podcast.

If you're a guest, request a recording of the show and post it on the front page of your website.

Meetup Groups

I used to do a Meetup group weekly about how to do more sales and speaking. It was free to come and we'd have a turnout from just a few to 15 people. Whatever size we had, that group was interested and involved and connected me with a lot of new people and my circle of potential business grew much bigger.

What I found was, if people were thinking about hiring me to coach them in sales or speaking, they would come to the Meetup. It was a very easy way to meet me. It was very nonthreatening because I wasn't asking for a sale, I was actually giving information. They could come to the Meetup, get a feel for me as a person, and decide whether they wanted to progress in working together.

I 'd know who wanted to work with me because they'd typically they'd hang around after the meeting and ask me more detailed questions about how I work or they'd just flat say, "How can I hire you? How can we work together?"

Blog

Use a blog to educate your prospects and provide valuable, useful information that actually solves people's problems, and makes a difference in their life. People will get to know you and then they'll want to work with you.

Make Yourself Available

The most successful people are the most available and accessible people. As Anthony Robbins says, "Proximity is power." Get close to the people you want to serve.

Suppose you want to specialize in working with condo buyers and sellers. Find out who the most helpful and influential people in that condominium complex are, serve them somehow. They'll do the referring for you, and because they know everybody in the building, they'll know who's going to sell or who's getting ready to, and they'll put a bug in that person's ear to hire you.

SECTION 3:
PERSUADE

Chapter 16:
The How To Talk To Buyer And Sellers Sales Program

The How to Talk to Buyers and Sellers Sales Program is designed to maximize your sales opportunities, and it's 9 steps that, if followed, lead to great results and can help you to create deep and lasting relationships, superior service, referrals, develop clients into raving fans who refer you like crazy and your sphere of influence becomes like a tribe that creates business and sales almost effortlessly.

On the other hand, if you don't have a sales system, you're probably winging it, and if these 9 steps are not followed it could result in upset prospects, lost revenue and no referrals.

I've been using this system and I recently had a client say, "I don't know why I'm doing this, but it's like my mission is to help your business grow."

I believe it's because this communication system works, and this is a communication system that I work when I'm speaking on stage, when I'm writing marketing, appearing on media and it's a system I definitely use for one-to-one sales.

The How to Talk to Buyers and Sellers Sales Program

Step 1: Success the First Second

Step 2: Seek safety

Step 3: Set the Hook

Step 4: Search Out Aims and Objectives

Step 5: Sell With Their Permission

Step 6: Slide What You Are Offering...Into Their Crosshairs

Step 7: Support Them...in Getting What They Want

Step 8: Save Shoppers 3 Through 9

Step 9: Shrink the Returns and Regrets

Any sales process is about cleaning up the stage, building rapport, finding out what they want, and helping them to get it. If you'll notice, at no point at all in the process was there a step like, "Pushing your product or service on them," or "convince people who don't want it to buy." Pushy sales are from a bygone era and people don't want them anymore.

So, what does work today?

Client centered service. Create a mindset of helping your prospect get a better life whether they ever work with you or not.

Step 1: Success the First Second

If there's a white elephant in the room, you need to address it. If you don't address it, it's going to make the rest of your sales presentation muddled and murky and you probably won't get the deal.

For example, when I was starting off as a new real estate professional, I had a listing appointment, and it was my biggest one yet. As I started my presentation a feeling of "Uh-oh" came over me, and I just had this sneaking suspicion, a gut feeling they were just shopping me to get ideas of what their house should sell for, and weren't serious about hiring me. They mentioned they had a friend who was an agent and I got this really strong vibe that they were going to list with their friend.

Instead of going on and pushing against their decision, I stopped the meeting early on, and said "Hey guys, if you just want my opinion on what the home is worth, I'll give you that. If you've already chosen someone to list it, let's just not waste your time or mine. But, if you're willing to let me have the opportunity to win your business, I'd like to show you what I can do."

Because I cleaned up the space early on, they actually gave me the chance to show them what I could do and they wound up listing the home with me, which was awesome.

Sometimes you'll make a mistake, and if you don't clean up the space you might never get the relationship off the ground. Let's suppose your car breaks down and you're late to meet a new prospect. If you don't address the tardiness, they're going to be thinking about, "Why was this person late?" and it will gnaw at them the entire time and they will not truly be listening to you or getting to know you.

If it's super-hot and their air conditioning is broken and you're sitting around the table trying to pretend everything's fine, and you don't address it they're going to be "in their head" about how hot it is and your presentation won't go well. Just say, "Wow, it is hot in here...and I'm committed that no matter what we get your house marketed and sold. Can we both be hot and still get this done?"

There's not always going to be a white elephant in the room, but if there is you need to address it.

Step 2: Seek safety
Go beyond just "Gaining rapport," and seek to create an interaction that is safe, supportive and enjoyable for both your prospect and you. We call it "Seek Safety."

In this step you want to create a safe place by understanding and talking to the personality type of your prospect, using the correct word patterns and using your physicality to create rapport.

Most sales trainings teach to gain rapport by "Talking about things you have in common." That technique works, but not for everybody. What's better is to talk to people they way they like talking. You've got to know different personality types and then speak the language they like.

Understanding personality types is an important part of 'gaining rapport'. Discover the personality type in the prospect and then give them the information the way they want it. Get to the point, or make it fun, or build the relationship or go with all the details. To help you learn how to do so, I want to share a bit of my product "Million Dollar Personality Power," - a personality types training with an emphasis on sales.

Identification

A beautiful part about knowing personality types is that you can identify with whom you're working over the phone or in person. As I go through the types I'll give you some quick nuggets on each type.

You want to identify who they are on the phone, so you'll have the best chance to act appropriately when you meet them in person, at which time you'll really be able to read them.

You must get out of your head, and over your concern for how your presentation will go and focus on them and read what kind of personality type they are instantly. You've got maybe 30 seconds to a minute to do so, because if you don't instantly read their body language, dress, house, and extrapolate their correct personality type, thereby communicating with them the wrong way, you could completely lose the deal before you have a chance to present. When you communicate to them in the ways their personality type likes, you've got a great chance to get the deal!

Give Information in the Way they Receive it Best

What we find is that most agents give information the way they want to receive information; so agents who love details go through everything methodically. When they do that with a prospect who wants bullet points and fun, their prospect's eyes are rolling back in their head and the prospect is bored to tears. The prospect will just want to get out of there and, they won't want to work with the agent, and they definitely don't refer them.

Agents who want to get it done quick will be that way with all prospects, and if they have a slower moving prospect they'll bowl them over and kill the relationship and leave a trail of bruised feelings and lost deals.

The Accommodator

7 out of 10 people you meet will be Accommodators, they're most concerned with the relationship.

Accommodators over the phone.
They'll be warm, emotional and slower paced compared to the Controllers and Passionates.

They'll spend time asking about you and expect the same, as they are relationship based. They're indirect, and they're going to ask you a lot of questions. They're not going to make demands. If they ask you a question they really mean it. If they ask you if 5:00pm is okay, they're really asking you if 5:00pm is okay ... and they probably feel like they've imposed on you even if 5:00 is perfect for you.

Accommodator phone strategy
Take your time. Answer all their questions. Spend time on the relationship and create the next steps together. Ask them how they'd like to proceed and make soft suggestions.

Accommodators are often married to Controllers, so make sure to ask "Who else will be involved in making this decision," to find out if there's another party involved. If there is, DO NOT present to the Accommodator alone; they'll try to make your presentation to the Controller, they won't do as good a job as you, and you most likely won't get the deal.

Accommodators in Person
Accommodators will be dressed for comfort. They'll approach slower, with a warm smile. They just feel comfortable to be around. They'll probably offer you a drink, or even a slice of pie.

Accommodators at Home
You'll see lots and lots of pictures of the family. A more "Homey" feel with comfortable furniture. There'll be a conspicuous absence of awards and plaques (unless they belong to their spouse, which they do. People tend to marry

their personality opposite. More on how to handle this later). They may have a mini-van or a practical car.

Accommodator Sales and Rapport Strategy

Take your time. Slow down. Do make sure to ask Accommodators about their family and how this decision will affect the family. Check to see if they are the one making the decision or if anyone else is involved - they'll usually defer to or involve others.

It's important to take care of any client, but especially the Accommodator - when they work with you they are expressing a level of faith and trust in you. Earn it and keep it.

Unlike the Controller, if you're talking to an accommodator and you get right down to work without establishing rapport, what will happen is the accommodator will say "yes, yes, yes" the whole meeting. You'll think everything's going great, and then they either won't sign with you or they'll kill it later, because they didn't want to hurt your feelings face to face, and they just didn't feel comfortable.

The Controllers

Controllers want results. Think about the prototypical CEO that's all results, results, results. Focusing on results is the ultimate controller attitude. They want results and they are direct about getting them.

If you go over to a controller's house and you start talking about the kids, the weather and you waste a bunch of time (that's how they'll receive it, wasting time) you'll lose the deal. Try gaining rapport that way, and they're going to kick you out.

Controllers are very action oriented, and they're very bottom-line driven. You'll be able to tell it's a controller over the phone by their very strong voice, demands, they're going to seem a little bit pushy, state their goals quickly and get down to business fast. They're going to try and control the conversation and if they ask questions the question is rhetorical or just to get what they want. They're more asking by phrasing a demand in the way of a question, such as "You can you meet at 5pm can't you?"

Controller phone strategy
Get their details and goals and close for the appointment quickly. Get an appointment as soon as possible because when the controller is ready to go they won't wait for you.

Controller in person
In person you'll recognize them by their strong presence, fast walk, strong handshake with a firm look in the eye and dressed to impress or dressed to get the job done.

At their home they'll have awards, plaques, diplomas and trophies on the wall. Their home will be well kept, usually by someone they've hired.

Controller Sales and Rapport Strategy
Get to the point, get it done, be fast and effective. Don't hold back and don't hide anything. The controllers want results fast. You need to get down to work right away. State why you're there in the first 30 seconds or they are booting you out.

The Passionate
Passionates seek fun, relationship and to look good. They want results paired with relationship.

Over the phone they'll have inflection in their voice, will spend some time getting to know you and they'll probably crack some jokes. They will have an opinion on what they want to accomplish and will let you know about it - probably including how neighbor so-and-so sold for X amount and they, "Should get AT LEAST that much."

Passionate Phone Strategy

Compliment, let them look good, keep it simple, light and fun and close quick

In person you'll recognize them by their energy, big smiles and colorful or "Notice me," clothes. Side note: many real estate professionals are Passionates. They'll approach you to say hi, and hold out their hand for a handshake with a big smile, or may just go in for the hug right away.

You'll recognize them at their home by their art, photos of where they've been, and probably a fair amount of clutter. If they lose their keys they're probably a Passionate.

Passionate Sales and Rapport Strategy
Enter with a huge smile, keep to bullet points, compliments, make it fun and close quick, not so they can get the "Result" but so they can get the work done and get back to having fun.

With "Passionate's," you've got to make it fun. You've got to keep it high energy, because if you don't you'll lose the deal.

The Planner
They want it done right and perfect. The Planner is indirect and they're very task-based.

Planner on the Phone.
The planner will have an even, monotone voice, and will talk quietly. They're not going to be real warm or asking questions to develop a relationship. The conversation will focus on the task that needs to be done.. They'll ask for details. "5:02 or 5:01? What time will you be there?" They're going to be very detail oriented and use a very flat voice.

Ask what details they'd like to see at the meeting and what info they'd like to read. Make it clear you'll proceed at their pace.

Planner Sales Strategy:

Give lots of details. Lots. Use "Standard operating procedure." Take your time. The best plan for planners may be to email or bring a lot of literature and leave it with them to read through. Plan on closing a Planner only after they've had time to think through the options and learn all about the process.

Frankly, in the same time it takes you to close one planner, you could close 4 or 5 controllers or passionates. Approach the transaction like you're solving a problem and get them involved to help solve it.

In summary, the planner will take forever. With the planners, you'll have to leave all your stuff there overnight and let them think about it.

Create Safety Through Your Words
If there's a certain jargon used in your farm area, get to know it and use it. If the condo building uses shorthand vernacular learn it before your meeting.

As your prospect expresses their desires and goals, echo those same words back to them. For example, if it's a buyer and they want space to raise a healthy family, don't talk about a home's "Prestige," talk about its "Space," and how it will help with the family.

Create Safety Through Your Body Language
Use your body to subtly mirror and match the body language of your prospect. Don't exactly mirror them, they'll see what you're doing and it will have the opposite of intended effect. Learn how to smoothly move into a space of rapport.

Create Safety Through Your Emotional State
If your prospect is timid and slow and your come in brash and fast, you'll blow them out. Instead, meet them where they are, and then after you've gained rapport, stair step them to a better emotional state by slowly shifting yours to the desired state.

What is the best emotional state for your client? The one they want. In step 4 you'll learn how to get your clients into the emotional state that will give the best chance for you to make the sale. Until that happens, the best state, as a rule of thumb, is eager and confident. We recommend you do the inner work on yourself to cultivate a state of eagerness and especially confidence. Emotional states are contagious, and if you're confident, they'll feel confident about working with you and won't even know why.

Step 3: Set the Hook
Have you ever tried to make a listing presentation and the kids are running around screaming, the TV is on, the phone's ringing and your prospect's attention is anywhere but with you? If you haven't, just imagine it. How do you think that listing appointment is going to go? I've been there, and the answer is not very well.

Let me correct that: I've been there before I learned Step 3: Set the Hook.
Setting the Hook means you're getting your prospect's attention so that you have a chance to sell them during your longer presentation.

As an illustration, let me share what I do as a speaker. When I take the stage the audience has 3 questions going through their head - and it's the same 3 questions your prospect has (whether a buyer or seller).
1. Is this for me?
2. Will this help me get what I want?
3. Do I like this person?

To set the hook at the beginning of my presentation I say the following, and I'd say it whether I'm presenting to one or one thousand (now keep in mind, I'll be selling sales training, after this example I'll do one for real estate).

"After 9/11 I went through a 6 month period where I made a total of $2,000 in commissions. Does anyone think that's a lot of money? No? Good. Then, using the information I came to share today, I learned how to create $96,000 in sales in 90 minutes. Would you like to know how I did it?"

This gets the audience's attention. It's a "Wow," that they want in their life, so it excites their subconscious and makes them want to tune in for the rest of the presentation.

Example for Real Estate.
When you talk with your prospect on the phone, it's effective to ask what their main goals are, so that when you walk in to the face to face meeting you'll be able to tailor your presentation to them.

Suppose it's September and your prospect says, "I'm transferring to another state, and we want to buy there, so we need to sell for X amount in order to have enough for a new home. Also, I'm being transferred sooner than expected and we'd like to be settled by Christmas for the kids."

You now know they want to sell in time and for enough to buy a new place, and be in by Christmas. When you start your presentation you'll say:

"If I could show you how to list and sell your home, for as much as possible, in the next 60 days, so that you'll buy a new home and be settled by Christmas so your kids can have great Christmas memories, would you be interested?"

Or, you can preface it with the phrase "Imagine..."

"Imagine we've done what it took to list and sell this house in the next 60 days for as much as possible: we've sold it for enough so that you'll be able to buy the perfect new home. Now imagine you're in and the home is ready for Christmas. How would that be? If you'd like to learn how to we can do it, stand by because I'm about to share how..."

The point of this step is NOT to make promises, but to get them to listen. Maybe you can or can't promise to sell in 60 days, for enough to buy at their destination. If you're a good agent, you can definitely share how to have the best chances for success and doing just that.

Step 4: Search Out Aims and Objectives

It's not about you.
It's not about your services.
It's not about how many people you have helped.
It's not about your office.
Repeat after me, "It's not about me."
It's about them. It's about your prospect. It's about what they want, what they need, what will improve their life.

The most important thing you can do when setting up your sale is find out the aims and objectives of your prospect.

Just in case it didn't sink in, here it is again: it's not about you.

Also, it's not just about what your prospect wants on a conscious level. It's also about what's in their heart: their subconscious needs and desires.

Too many people go to a sales presentation and they give information. They do it all on a conscious level ... "Here's what we do; here's why we're the best."

Nobody cares and it doesn't sell.

Instead, find out what your prospect wants on both a conscious and a subconscious level.

Here's an example of how this showed up in my life.

A few years ago I was moving and I hired someone to help me find a place. We looked and looked and looked, couldn't find a place that worked for me.

Then I realized she only asked me what I wanted on a conscious level. I said "3 bedrooms, 2 bathrooms and I'd like to have a pool." That was it, what my conscious mind answered: I was speaking from my mind, not my heart, and we couldn't find a place that works.

Then I realized that she never asked the questions to discover what I really wanted. She either didn't know how, or didn't know the importance of, finding out what was in my heart. She never asked the questions that would have me produce the answers that would help her find the right place, and give me enough emotional juice to move and say, "Yes."

Please memorize this statement, ***"All buying decisions begin in the heart and are backed up by the brain."***

We had been looking for weeks, and I was frustrated, so I decided to find out for myself what I really wanted. But how would I do it? I'd use on myself what I call the "4th Level Question," a sales technique composed of a series of questions that help you discover the subconscious motivators for your client.

In the 4th Level Question Technique you drill down to what's in your client's heart, and discover what's really important to them on a conscious and more importantly, emotional (subconscious) level.

I'm asked myself, "Why is a 3 bedroom, 2 bath with a pool important to me?"

What I discovered was that the 3 bedrooms represented for me a separate place to have my home-based business, a place to have friends come visit and stay over, a room to make my own, and the pool represented fun.

So why was all that important to me?

Well, I wanted to grow my business, so I needed a place to work from that would give me a room to expand my life and my business. Friends represented love and connection, and the fun of the pool represented a place to unwind after working hard.

Really what I was looking for wasn't a 3 bedroom, 2 bath. I was looking for a place for growth, connection, love, fun and unwinding.

When I got clear on growth, connection, love, fun and unwinding, and understood that's what I really wanted...I found a place within 48 hours.

When you're going to work with someone to help them buy or sell, if you'll take the time to sit down and go through these questions that are designed to discover the conscious, and the subconscious needs of your prospect, you'll be serving them in a way no one else serves them.

What are the benefits to you? Happier clients, faster buyers, and more referrals to name a few. There are also exclusive buyer representation agreements and more listings.

Some real estate professionals are afraid to ask for an exclusive buyer representation agreement. If you are serving them, and finding out what they want on the subconscious level, they'll be happy to sign an exclusive buyer representation agreement because nobody else is asking them the same questions you are. Nobody else will be seen to care as much as you do. Nobody else will be finding out what they really want. Nobody else can offer what you can offer: to help them get what they want most.

If you're talking to someone who's listing and you find out on the subconscious level what it represents for them and what would be the ultimate outcome for them ... they're probably going to sign with you that night because it will be so clear to them what they want, and that they can get it with you. Why don't they feel this way about other agents? You're the only person asking them these questions. You're the only one serving their heart.

How to do the 4th Level Question:
Ask them, "If this went perfect, whether you think it's realistic or not, or we can do it or not, what would happen, what would it be like?"

As they answer you make sure to take notes, and write down specific words they use.

Usually to start this conversation is they'll give you all their conscious wants and needs, the top of mind things like 3 bedrooms 2 baths, with a pool in such and such neighborhood

They Give Important Things In Order
When people tell you what they want, they'll automatically list their desires in descending order, starting with the most important. The most important thing will be listed first, followed by the 2nd most important, 3rd most important, 4th most important, 5th most important etc

If you go back to my example I named:
3 bedrooms
2 baths
pool

That's it. I didn't name a neighborhood because it wasn't important to me. I said 3 bedrooms first because it was more important to me than a pool.

4th Level Question Step 2

Say, "What I heard you say was..." and repeat what they said. If you missed it or got it wrong, correct it.

After you've captured their answer from step 1, you'll ask, "Why is _____ (what they said in step 1) important to you?"

Write down their answers.

4th Level Question Step 3

At this point you've asked a lot of questions, probably more than most people would ask, and your prospect is either wondering where this is going, or getting emotional (which is good) or both.

To reassure them say, "I know this is a lot of questions, and it may sound redundant or obvious, and I believe if I am to truly serve you I have to serve what's in your head and your heart, and to do that I want to ask these questions, so stick with me, OK?"

Now you'll say, "What I heard you say was _____ (answers from step 2). Why is _____ (the answers you got in step 2 important to you?"

Write down the answers

4th Level Question Step 4

At this point they're already talking to you from the heart and opening up about their life...or they're about to!

Now you'll say again, "What I heard you say was _____ (answers from step 3). Why is _____ (the answers you got in step 3 important enough to you to take action on it right now?"

By now they'll be speaking from the heart, and you can expect a few tears...from them as well. I find that when my prospect really opens up to me in Step 3 or 4 something inside me switches on and I have so much more compassion, caring and desire to take care of them. We're made to be compassionate and this step really switches it on.

Once you've discovered what they really want, from the heart, in step 3 or 4, you now know how to serve them best.

4th Level Question Step 5: Tie down the emotions to you.
Tie it all up and say, something to the effect of..

Agent: "Awesome! I can get behind that. My goal, when we work together is to get you _____ (what they said they want, from the heart, in Step 4).

Agent: When you work with me you can count on me working with you towards the goal of creating those _____ (one or two things from Step 4 that really touched you).

4th Level Question Example
Let's suppose we're speaking with someone considering listing with us. Below is the agent and prospect's conversation, with comments.

4th Level Question Step 1
Agent: "If this went perfect, whether you think it's realistic or not, or we can do it or not, what would happen, what would it be like?"

Prospect: "I'd sell fast, for top dollar and buy up."

Remember, your prospect will give conscious desires in descending order of importance. To serve this person well, you'd keep in mind that a fast sale is more important than top dollar or buying up, and that top dollar is more important than buying up.

4th Level Question Step 2

Agent: What I heard you say was you'd sell fast, for top dollar and buy up. Is that correct?

Prospect: Yes

Agent: Why is selling fast, for top dollar and buying up important to you?"

Prospect: My wife just got pregnant, and we need to move before she gets too far along.
NOTE: The prospect only answered why selling fast was important, so the agent will still need to ask about top dollar and buying up.

Agent: Why is top dollar important?

Prospect: With the kid on the way she will work less, we'll have more bills and who knows what may happen.

Agent: and buying up?

Prospect: I'd like to have the room to not have to move again for a while and I'd like more kids.

4th Level Question Step 3
Agent: What I heard you say was that your wife just got pregnant, and you need to move before she gets too far along. With your kid on the way she will work less, you'll have more bills and you don't know what else may happen. I also heard you say you'd like to have more kids and have the room to not have to move again for a while.

Prospect: Yes, that's right. You're awesome! Nobody else asked me that.

At this point you've demonstrated more care and consideration than most other agent. Most agents just jump into their presentation and what they do, very few find out what's important to their prospect.

You've asked a lot of question, definitely more than most, so to make it ok to ask more say, "I know this is a lot of questions, and it may sound redundant or obvious, and I believe if I am to truly serve you, I have to serve what's in your head *and* your heart, and to do that I have to ask these questions, so stick with me, OK?"

Prospect: OK

Agent: I know the answer may be obvious to you and I want to see what's really important to you - why do you need to move before she gets too far along? Also, what concerns you with not knowing what will happen with money? Why is having more kids and room important to you?

Prospect: She had difficulty with the last one and we don't want to take chances. I'm concerned about the money because when I was a kid we didn't have a lot and I want my kids to have more than I did. I want to have more kids because that's what I grew up with, and more room because I want to work from home more and I don't want them driving me crazy.

4th Level Question Step 4
Agent: Ok, last round of questions.
What I heard you say was that she had difficulty with the last one, and I'm so sorry to hear that, and that you don't want to take chances. You're concerned about the money because when you were a kid you didn't have a lot and you want your kids to have more than you did. You said you want to have more kids because that's what you grew up with and more room because you want to work from home more and you don't want them driving you crazy.

Agent: Is that right?

Prospect: Yes.

Agent, OK, last question. You said you want to sell fast, not take chances on the pregnancy, make sure your kids have more than you had, have more kids because that's what you grew up with and more room because you want to work from home more and you don't want them driving you crazy.

Agent: Why is all that important enough to you to take action on it right now?"

Prospect: It's been my lifelong dream to live in a beautiful home with a big family, and all be together during the holidays. I never thought I could afford it. I can and now is the time. If I'm going to give my kids great memories, now is the time to do it. Also, my wife is amazing and I want to give her the best I can. She deserves it.

4th Level Question Step 5

Agent: Awesome! I can get behind that. My goal, when we work together is to get you into that beautiful home that will let your big family be together during the holidays, so you can give your kids great memories, and so you can give your amazing wife the best.

Agent: When you work with me you can count on me working with you towards the goal of creating those memories.

What to Do With the Information You've Gained: Align or Move On

You will have discovered what is really important to your prospect, and if you're doing it right, both you and your prospect may be in tears. When you hear a prospect talk about what's really important to them, it's usually easy to align with supporting your prospect in getting it. Most people have very inspiring dreams and goals - and you may find yourself working even harder and smarter for them.

What do you do if you can't support what your prospect wants? What do you do if their goals are contrary to yours?

Let's take a situation of where your Prospect's desires and goals, are to you, inappropriate. It may be very difficult to work with them, and you have a choice to make.

Your choices at the end of Step 4:

1. You're already aligned - do everything you can to get the deal.

2. Go from not aligned to aligned with your prospect: give up your values, or in the name of service, make them secondary to your prospects' value.

3. Don't align, and still serve them as a way to speak something better into their lives. Love and serve them as a way to be around them, and earning a chance to influence them to change for the better.

4. Leave them alone. Just decline the opportunity and move on.

5. Refer them to another agent. Find an agent who will be a better fit for them and refer the agent and make a referral fee.

Which should you do? Do you pray? That's the first step I'd take.

Frankly, I understand that you may need the money and it would be very hard to pass on a client. Here's some food for thought - one difficult client can sap so much time, energy and money that you'll regret it in the end - and quite often they don't close. On the other hand, some people, when served with love, change and become your biggest fans and referral sources.

I wish I could tell you what to do, and I can tell you this...when you're aligned it's super exciting and fun to work with your client, now move on to Step 5!

Step 5: Sell With Their Permission

Now that you've discovered what they want, you'll open the door to selling smoothly and naturally by telling a story, and if you have it, showing a testimonial.

In step 4 you discovered your prospects' conscious and subconscious desires. You'll link their desires to your offer through the story you tell in Step 5.

NOTE: We have not talked about your product or services until Step 5. Why? Because it's not important. Well, it's not important until you know what they want.

How in the world can you help someone get what they want before you know what they want?

Now say, "Before I go on, let me share a quick story," and tell a story that fits what your prospect wants. Tell a story of a person who was in the same position as your client, a story that illustrates you can help your prospect get what they want. For instance, if they are looking to list for top dollar and move out of state, tell a story about a client you helped who listed, sold well and moved out of state.

Leverage Stories from Collective Experience

Where will you get the stories? From your life, the life of a client you've worked with, true stories from your broker, agents, transaction coordinators or other people in your office and tell those stories.

Imagine working with an empty nester that wants to downsize. After you've found out what they want, then tell a story about an empty nester who had huge success working with you or someone in your office.

If you're new or newer to the area, you can leverage off the authority of your office. You could say, " I work with such and such an office, and I'd like to share with you the story about someone who is in your position and what we did for them..." List out everything you or your office did, how it was a huge success, and if you have it show a written or video testimonial.

Step 5 Summary: Link to Step 6, and get their permission to talk about your services.
In Step 5 Sell With Their Permission you'll share a story or show a testimonial to communicate to your prospect how you, or your office, helped someone exactly in your prospect's shoes.

Then, you're going to ask "Would you like to know how we could help you get ___ (what they said they wanted in a what they are buying or selling Step 4) and make sure you get ____ (emotional desires) and the transaction is _____ (how their personality type would like it: fast, fun, cover all the details or we're doing it together) would you be interested in hearing how?"

They're going to say, "Yeah, that would be awesome," and the door is open to present your service.

Example
Would you like to know how we could help you get a 3/2 and make sure you have room to grow, relax and that the transaction is fun, would you be interested in hearing how?

Step 6: Slide What You Are Offering...Into Their Crosshairs
Here's where you begin to present your actual services, and because of what you've discovered, the way, or the context, in which you present your services will be most effective.

Present to the personality type of your prospect (Controller, Passionate, Planner or Accommodator) and talk about how you provide what's most important to them (fast, fun, details and processes, or together).

When you present "What," you do, and "How," you do it, make sure to frame your services within the context of the emotional drivers of your prospect, which you've discovered in Step 4 through the 4th Level Question.

It's best to provide what your prospect said they wanted in Step 4 Search Out Aims and Objectives.

Step 7: Support Them...in Getting What They Want
This is what most, "Sales trainers," call the Close. We call it Creating New Futures: when you sell someone on your services you're creating a new, better, future for two parties and at least two people: your client and you.

Your New Future: When you create a deal, you're fulfilling on your Mission, you're serving a fellow human, you're making the money to support what you're up to in life, you're creating the resources for your dreams, goals, family and fun, and you're growing something great in your business.

Your Client's New Future: Are there agents who don't care as much as you? Are there agents who are not as qualified as you, not as good as you, or even worse will use and abuse a Client? You are saving your new client from that future and they now have the new future of being cared for by an expert who will go above and beyond to serve them. They will also be creating what's important to them, because you'll be aligning with them in support of what they want (which you discovered in Step 4).

We call this *Support Them in Getting What They Want* because in this step your job is to do everything you can to help your prospect say, "Yes," and commit to getting what they want by moving from your prospect to your client.

Mindset of Supporting Them in Getting What They Want
You may find so much peace and relief from reframing the "Close" or "Asking for the sale," to taking the focus off you and putting 100% of your focus on your Prospect getting what they want.

Sure, you want the money, you want the commission, but if you focus there, you'll kill your sales.

Jase shared that when he speaks, if he takes the stage hoping to make a lot of money, the sales suffer. On the other hand, if he puts his focus on serving, he'll typically make many more sales.

It's tough to do - giving up what you want and trusting that you'll be provided for - and it's probably the best sales technique you can find.

Here's what Jase says to himself when he takes the stage:
> *"These people's lives will be better forever because I was here, whether they ever work with me or not."*

Your Presentation Goal in Step 7
Make it easy for your Prospect to say, "Yes."

We call it the Water-Slide Theory. What happens when you get on a water slide and push off? You go to the bottom, and usually fast. Once you get on the slide and push off there's little work to do, you just go along for the ride, and have fun.

Now imagine the beginning of Step 7 is your prospect pushing off, and the presentation is the slide, with the arrival at the bottom being your Prospect's, "Yes." That's what you want your sales process to be like: make it easy, fun, with little work for your prospect.

Ways to Make it an Easy "Yes."
Exclusivity
Limited Time Offer
Bonuses
Fast Action Bonuses

Use Million Dollar Language
Now during this entire time you want to be using "million dollar language." It's a form of programming language or success language; the way you talk to yourself and the way you talk to others. Our words are like seeds. The seeds we speak go into people's ears and they take root in their heart, and then they sprout a plant or a tree.

The fruit of that tree is based on what seeds were planted. If you want apples to grow you need to plant apple seeds. If you want oranges to grow you need to plant orange seeds.

So, if we want a client to take action we need to plant seeds of taking action the entire time we're speaking to them and every time we're speaking to them. This is very similar to neuro-linguistic programming.

Some agents will plant seeds of doubt and fear, and so their clients or prospects are filled with doubt and fear. Other ones will plant seeds of confidence, abundance, saying yes, taking action fast, and people will feel confident, abundant, say yes and take action fast.

So, go study language patterns!

When you're going for the "close," instead of calling it "closing," call it "creating new futures" because if they work with you, they can have a new vision of their future.

Many for sale by owner types don't think they can afford a real estate professional or they are too afraid to work with one, Often, the truth is that they would have made more money working with a real estate professional. Because they never hired an agent and they went into foreclosure, they were worse off than if they had hired a real estate professional.

When you have the tools of persuasion, you can sell people and make their life better. It creates a new future for them because they have a better life, and it creates a new future for you because now you have this new client that you're going to work with.

Everybody truly wins in this kind of a transaction. It's called, "creating a new future."

One, you want to know how to read body language. Think about a first kiss. If you try and go for the kiss too soon you're going to lose that kiss. If you wait too long, you miss the buying signal ...you're going to lose that kiss.

You've got to know when to go for it, and it's the same with a transaction. If you close too fast you'll lose the deal. If you close too late you're going to lose the deal. You've got to know how to read the signals to back off or to progress ahead.

Buying Signals to Look for

* If they touch or fondle the home.
* If they're a planner type they're going to ask you questions.
* If they're asking, "Is this in our price range?" or if they ask almost any question about the house or the home, that's a buying signal.
* If you put the contract on the table and they pick it up and look at it, that's a buying signal. So, anytime they touch it or take a better look, they're interested.

Then, to get them to actually say yes, = make saying yes an easy choice. Make it an easy decision. Show the pain and cost of waiting. Show how taking action now is better and then also make it as secure of a process as you can.

If it's a listing, give them as much guarantee as you can, such as maybe they can back out if they're not happy with your product or service. If you're going to be serving them well, they're not going to back out, right? Giving any guarantee you can will be effective to help close that deal.

Understanding personality types and buying signals will go a long way in creating success for your business, but learning how to maximize your time and close more deals is the true basis for tripling, 4X, or even increasing your income 6X more or greater with the same amount of effort. In the next chapter you will learn a new way of thinking to help you close more deals and increase your income with the same effort you are making now.

Step 8: Save Shoppers 2 Through 9

Chapter 17:
Close More Deals

Close More Deals—Make More Money With the Same Effort
One of the steps in the persuasion paradigm shows you what is called "Save Shoppers 2 through 9."

You may find peace in knowing that if you go on enough appointments, approximately one out of 10 people will say, "Yes" to you.

In my experience you'll always get at least 10% of your prospects to turn into clients. I mean, if you stink, you should still get one out of 10 sales. They'll just say, "Yes," to you. Maybe you remind them of their grandson, they're desperate, you were highly referred, they think you're cute or who knows what.

On the other hand, one out of 10 will always say no. You can't consistently close 100% of the people. You're too new, too experienced; your office is too big, too small, blah, blah, blah. Someone will always say, "No," just get used to it and move on.

What is important is what you do with the other 8 out of 10 opportunities.

How much do you want to make?
Do you want more time?
Would you like to make more money in less time?
If you said, "Yes," then you need to Save Shoppers 2 Through 9.

**We like to say,
The money is made in the middle!**

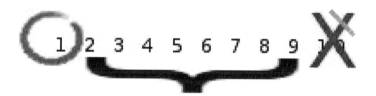

This is where the money is made!

Average agents, seem to have limited opportunities to grow, they barely make it, or go out of business. Profitable agents make more money, and they may seem to have more opportunities, but it may not be so. Each agent (unless the average one quits) will eventually go on 10 appointments, the difference between the two is that while the average agent closes one out of 10, the profitable agent has learned how to Create New Futures and will get 4, 5, 6 or more deals out of 10.

How good your persuasion skills are dictates whether you go on 10 appointments and you get 1 out of 10, 2 out of 10, 3 out of 10...or up that, 7, 8 or 9 out of 10.

Communication Equals Wealth

Milton Erikson said, "Communication equals wealth." Your communication with yourself and the outside world, dictates how much money you make, how happy you are, how much time you have available for what you really care about.

Get a 50 to 70% Close Rate

It's very reasonable for people to improve their communications skills and expect to get 50 to 70% close rate; especially if you've done everything else we've talked about with the prepositioning and the research and the videos, the testimonials.

When you put all that together, you can get that 60%, 70% close rate.

The Value of the Middle

Would you like to double, triple or even quadruple your income with more time off? Save Shoppers 2 through 9!

If you're currently closing 10%, and you learn how to close 50% of your appointments, instead of going on 10 appointments and getting 1, you could go on only 8 appointments and get 4 deals. That's 4 times your income, and you have more time available because you're going on 2 less appointments (or go on those 2 appointments and make even more money in the same amount of time).

Triple Your Income

What if they go on 5 appointments and they close 3?

Many agents don't have the time for the things that are important to them, like their family their kids or vacations. If these agents learned how to persuade, they could go on 5 appointments and close 3 deals where they used to go on 10 and close 1.

In other words, they just tripled their income in half the time.

They have 3 times as much money, and more available time for what's important to them.

How To Get More Deals
How do you get more of the deals? Make it easy in Step 8, and re-close the middle again and again in Step 9.

Most agents ask for the deal once then bail; huge mistake. You must ask for the sale, whether a buyer or listing, over and over and over again. How many times do you ask? Until you die, they die, they hire another agent, or you risk damaging the relationship.

When I, Jase, was an ineffective agent, I would call a For Sale By Owner (FSBO) once to ask if they wanted to list. If they said, "No," I would never call them again. I'd do a listing appointment for the FSBO and if they said, "No" I'd say to myself, "Whew, I'm out of here. I'm one more no closer to yes!" Like I said, I was ineffective, but really I stunk.

When I learned how to sell I began asking the FSBOs for the sale over and over (and over) again. I'd call them. I'd do a listing presentation. I'd stop by to drop off info on the neighborhood. I'd see if there was something else they needed. I'd call them back once a week. I'd ask for their business over and over again. What happened to my business?

I got more deals in less time!

Vitamin B Gives You Energy and More Sales for Your Business
I learned something, too: energy begets energy, action begets action, and when you get on a roll it's not the time to quit, it's the time to turn it up!

Many ineffective or average agents get a deal, or get paid at a closing, and then they quit working on new business...and it's a huge mistake.

How do you feel when you get a new listing or buyer? You feel great. Do you have less confidence or more? More. Are you less excited about your business or do you feel on top of the world, like you're the best? You feel great like you're the woman, and you rock!

What's a better state to be in to close more deals?
A. Hoping to get a deal, average confidence, and so-so excitement about your business?
B. Feeling great, confident, excited, on top of the world, feeling great like you're the man and knowing you rock!

B is MUCH better.

So why do we act like an A? Why do we quit after getting a deal? Why do we take time off after getting paid? Probably because we're used to being average, and it's what the average agent does.

It really doesn't matter why. What matters is that you give it up and take some vitamin B. Be like type B and when you get on a roll, keep going and you're setting yourself up for closing more deals.

Type B:
Get a listing, and immediately call the FSBO down the street (and if you want say, "I just listed a home down the street from you. We find that having two or more houses for sale in the same neighborhood helps each sell faster and for more. Are you ready to list and get this knocked out?!) and in your 'up' state you'll have so much confidence and energy it will be contagious for the home owner and they'll be more open to meeting with you.

Have a solid closing scheduled for the afternoon? Do a presentation in the morning - you'll be up, excited and present better because you'll know that no matter how this presentation goes, you're getting paid that afternoon.

Get a new Exclusive Buyer Representation Agreement signed? Call that FSBO and talk about how excited you are about real estate and how you're getting more and more buyers every day!

When you're on a roll, keep rolling!

Step 9: Shrink the Returns and Regrets

Save the Deal

When it comes to the actual closing, we talked about making it easy. You want to "save the deal." Even though they sign a contract, the deal's not done; pre-frame this too. Make your buyer's aware of this: "Buying a home is much like running hurdles. There's going to be a ton of hurdles between now and when this closes."

Learn to "Pre-frame" Things

Just signing the contract is when the excitement starts. Between contract and close is where you find the difficult challenges. When you set expectations with a buyer that there will be hurdles ahead, then one day when something goes wrong or something negative comes up...they'll looked at you and say, "Yeah, you told us this was coming. We're totally fine with it." They are ready to accept it.

On the other hand, if you don't pre-frame things, when the slightest thing comes up that is a negative, the buyer might say, "Uh, let's just cancel this. It's too hard." Pre-framing the situation the right way makes all the difference.

Offer a Buyer's Remorse Kit

Think about offering a "buyer's remorse kit," especially for buyers. Take a piece of chocolate and wrap it up, and you say "In case of emergency, open this." Tell the buyer, "Hey listen, if you ever get really stressed or you're ever thinking about cancelling this deal or you're worried, I want you to open this and then call me".

"Pattern Interrupt"
What happens is when they open it, is it interrupts them. It's called a "pattern interrupt," and then physically the chemicals in the chocolate change the biology in their body and in their thought process, they feel better, and they stay in the transaction.

Hand-holding vs. Canceling a Deal
95 out of 100 times, it's just that they're nervous ... it's something new and they just need a little bit of reassurance and handholding and they're going to be happy with the transaction.

All this of course is predicated on "you care about them more than you do about the money," because let's suppose the inspection comes back—termites or something, and the repairs aren't going to be covered by the seller and it's just such a bad deal for them now—you need to support them in doing the right thing for them no matter what.

If it's really in their best interests to cancel the deal, then you have to support them in canceling the deal, even when you need the commission.

Do The Right Thing for the Client Every Time

* One, you've got to be able to look at yourself in the mirror and feel good about yourself.

* Two, I believe we have a big man upstairs that's looking down and you want to do what's right for other people.

* Three, people feel it when you treat them right and it will come back to you.

In my last seminar this husband and wife bought an advanced package that we offer, and it was around $18,000 ... $18,000 to $20,000, but it turned out for what they wanted they only needed to buy 1, not 2. When I went over and said "Hey guys, it's only $10,000. You only have to buy 1, not 2," they were ecstatic and they were so impressed that I was willing to take $8,000 in sales off the table. It really cemented the honesty and the value of working with me.

Conclusion

In conclusion, you now have all of the tools and strategies that you need to build a highly successful real estate business.

You've learned secrets of top producing real estate professionals. Use this insider's guide to duplicate their success. Over 50 years' experience in real estate and interaction with over 400,000 agents have gone into making this book!

In this book, you've learned the difference between an effective and an ineffective agent, uncovered a proven system to develop the habits of an effective agent and become the #1 choice; drawing clients to you effortlessly. You've been given 3 daily activities that will rocket you to success and learned the 4 secret components to getting and completing sales.

Along the way, the three authors have shared their personal success systems and even their lessons learned from failure so that you can learn faster and build a better business.

We wish you a future full of learning and prosperity.